WATERSIDE WALKS
in
The Peak District

Charles Wildgoose

COUNTRYSIDE BOOKS
NEWBURY, BERKSHIRE

First published 2008
© Charles Wildgoose, 2008

COUNTRYSIDE BOOKS
3 Catherine Road
Newbury, Berkshire

To view our complete range of books,
please visit us at
www.countrysidebooks.co.uk

ISBN: 978 1 84674 080 0

Maps by Gelder Design & Mapping
Photographs by the author

Cover picture of Youlgreave bridge
supplied by Derek Forss

Designed by Peter Davies, Nautilus Design
Produced through MRM Associates Ltd., Reading
Typeset by Jean Cussons Typesetting, Diss, Norfolk
Printed by Information Press, Oxford

Contents

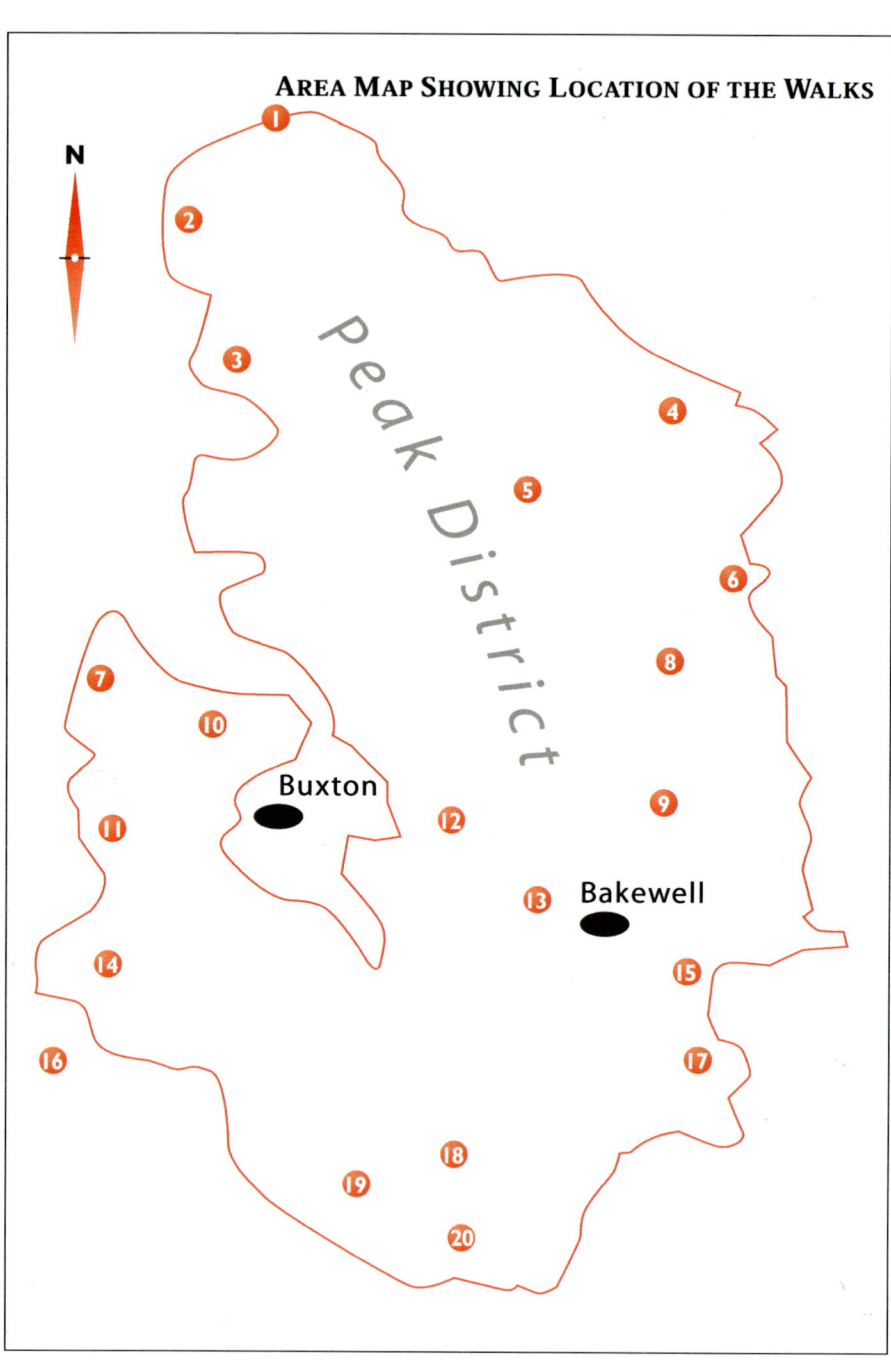

AREA MAP SHOWING LOCATION OF THE WALKS

N

Peak District

Buxton

Bakewell

PUBLISHER'S NOTE

We hope that you obtain considerable enjoyment from this book; great care has been taken in its preparation. Although at the time of publication all routes followed public rights of way or permitted paths, diversion orders can be made and permissions withdrawn.

We cannot, of course, be held responsible for such diversion orders and any inaccuracies in the text which result from these or any other changes to the routes nor any damage which might result from walkers trespassing on private property. We are anxious though that all details covering the walks are kept up to date and would therefore welcome information from readers which would be relevant to future editions.

The simple sketch maps that accompany the walks in this book are based on notes made by the author whilst checking out the routes on the ground. They are designed to show you how to reach the start, to point out the main features of the overall circuit and they contain a progression of numbers that relate to the paragraphs of the text.

However, for the benefit of a proper map, we do recommend that you purchase the relevant Ordnance Survey sheet covering your walk. The Ordnance Survey maps are widely available, especially through booksellers and local newsagents.

INTRODUCTION

Whether you're walking beside the Huddersfield Narrow Canal in the far north or strolling beside the river Dove in beautiful Dovedale in the south, there is so much splendid scenery for you to enjoy in the Peak District. Over 50 miles separates these two walks but all the walks in this book share the same theme – 'water'.

Twenty waterside walks required! That was the task set for me by Countryside Books and what an enjoyable one it proved to be. One of them may disappoint slightly because the river Manifold often dries up in summer but I think you will forgive a little latitude when you see the valley. Go to Grindon in autumn or winter, or after a prolonged stretch of heavy rain in summer, if you want to see the river – and it's still a splendid walk without the water!

Details are given as to how to get there, where to park and where to get something to eat and drink afterwards. Some of the car parks and the pubs and tea rooms get very busy in season so try and get an early start, just in case. And if you want to make a day of it, there are suggestions for places to visit nearby or things to do, such as a ride on a steam train or a trip on the canal.

A word of guidance if you will allow me. Whilst it is possible to follow these walks from the walk description and sketch map given, it is always worth taking the appropriate OS map with you, too, so that should you stray off the path, you have an additional reference.

All the walks have been checked and I'm indebted to my checkers. My thanks go to every one of them: Kath and Robert Walker, Pat, George and Emily Smith, Amy Wyles, James Hensman, Jo Parry, Robin Mills, Carole and Stuart Middleton, Di Carnell and Anna Tyrrell. A very special mention must go to Ruth, Graham and Thomas Rhodes who have walked all but one of the routes – thank you all very much. And, as ever, special thanks to Balkees. She has either walked or checked every single walk. Her input is always important and, at times of doubt, it is to her that I turn for advice.

There's some tremendous scenery to see in the Peak District and even with this, my eleventh book, I'm still finding routes I've never walked before. We are so very, very lucky to live in or near this part of the world.

Enjoy your walking.

Charles Wildgoose

MARSDEN AND THE HUDDERSFIELD NARROW CANAL

Fine views reward the effort of a couple of short, steepish climbs after walking up the valley from Marsden beside the Huddersfield Narrow Canal, Tunnel End Reservoir and an attractive stream.

Standedge tunnel and visitor centre

- **HOW TO GET THERE:** Marsden is on the A62 south-west of Huddersfield. Follow the signs for the railway station once you reach Marsden.
- **PARKING:** Drive up the cobbles to the right of the station, opposite the Railway pub. Bear right and park beyond the National Trust Estate Office.
- **LENGTH OF THE WALK:** 5¼ miles. Map: OS OL21 South Pennines (GR 047118).

After walking up the valley beside the canal, the (manageable) climb begins. After negotiating this, and enjoying the views, you then walk across the hillside looking down onto Marsden and over to the hills beyond. Coming back down into the valley, there is a final stroll of just under a mile beside the canal. The Huddersfield Narrow Canal stretches for 20 miles between Huddersfield and Ashton under Lyne, and at its summit is the highest navigable waterway in Britain. On the route you pass close to the Standedge Tunnel, built beneath the Pennines and the longest and highest canal tunnel in the country.

The Tunnel End Inn is passed on the route, but to return to it by car turn right on the road from the railway station and cross the road bridge. Immediately beyond turn left along Reddisher Road and continue until you reach the Inn on the right. This is a pub worth searching out. There's a very friendly welcome, the food is delicious and the beer excellent. The regulars are Black Sheep Bitter and Timothy Taylor Landlord, with guests like Springhead Bitter. Monday to Thursday they open in the evenings only but from Friday to Sunday they're open from 12 noon until 11 pm. Food is served from noon until 2.30 pm on Friday, until 3 pm on Saturday and until 4 pm on Sunday. There are a number of other pubs and tearooms in Marsden itself.

Telephone: 01484 844636; www.tunnelendinn.com.

THE WALK

1. With the Railway pub behind you and the railway line and canal in front, walk left with the Huddersfield Narrow Canal now on your right. Pass Lock 42E here. Proceed alongside the canal on your right, passing under a road bridge. Stay on the towpath as you get into the open. Pass under a railway bridge. Keep on beside the canal, then rise up to and cross the next bridge to get onto the far side. Turn left to see Standedge Tunnel. Pass a small car park on your left and walk up the access road which leads away from the Centre. This brings you to the Tunnel End Inn.

2. Turn left on the level road directly in front of the Inn. A few yards later turn left through a gate to reach Tunnel End Reservoir. Turn right almost immediately, keeping the reservoir on your left. Stay on the raised path with Waters Road on your right. Cross a bridge over a stream and continue up the valley. The path brings you out onto the lane.

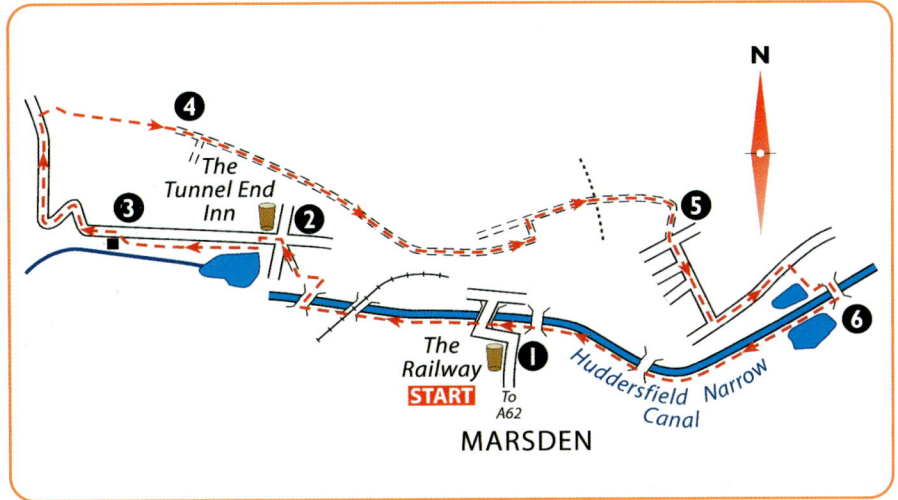

3. Turn left here, passing Trethella Cottage. You reach the main entrance to Hey Green on your right. Ignore the steps that lead to Lower Green Owlers, taking Blake Lea Lane to the left of the path. Follow this as it zigzags quite steeply before levelling out. You pass a property on the left. Then, 40 yards beyond a mast on your left, go through the right-hand gate of a pair on your right. Walk down into the valley away from the lane, following a track. Cross a footbridge and stay on the track as it wheels right – it can be very muddy here. The grassy track leads past the ruins of a couple of buildings. Keep forward on the level to reach a small gate. In the field beyond, proceed along the narrow path. Where the path forks, ignore the path to the left, taking the right fork to descend gradually. Head towards the gable end of a property ahead. Ignore any paths to the left. Pass through a gap, following the walled path, walking behind the building on your right.

4. You reach a tarmac lane. Follow this, passing another property on your left. The lane subsequently bends to the right. At the T-junction turn left along another lane. You then pass a farm on your right. Beyond this, at a cluster of six or seven properties, keep on the lane as it bears left. Tunnel End Reservoir should be visible a couple of fields downhill to your right. Pass another property, whereafter you should see a Kirklees Way waymark. At High Fall keep going and look out for views of Butterley Reservoir on the right. In 300 yards turn left (ignoring a path to the right), then 100 yards later turn right. Keep forward, ignoring the

The view of the valley and Tunnel End Reservoir

path that crosses the track you are on. You lose height and the track swings downhill.

5. On reaching a tarmac lane at a crossroads, descend for 300 yards to the road at the bottom. Turn left along this. Follow it for just under ½ mile, taking care as you go. After carefully negotiating a steepish section of road, with bends, take the path on the right for Sandhill Cottages. Walk down the track past the cottages and then a reservoir on the right. Proceed beside the canal on your right. Climb the steps to cross the footbridge over the canal. Turn left and keep left to get back down to the canal.

6. Now follow the canal all the way back to the start, keeping the water on your right. As you go you will pass a number of locks.

PLACES OF INTEREST NEARBY:

Visit the **Standedge Tunnel Visitor Centre**, which opened in 2001. At weekends and bank holidays there may be an opportunity to enjoy a canal boat ride from here too. Telephone: 01484 844298 (Easter to November) or 0113 281 6860 (off season).

Alternatively drive up to **Holme Moss**, over 1,700 ft above sea level, and admire the stupendous view from the car park.

UPPERMILL, THE HUDDERSFIELD NARROW CANAL AND THE RIVER TAME

A fairly easy walk with no strenuous climbs but plenty of interest. The other waterway on this walk is the river Tame, which is crossed by the canal via an aqueduct.

Walking beside the Huddersfield Narrow Canal

- **HOW TO GET THERE:** Uppermill is 5 miles to the east of Oldham on the A670.
- **PARKING:** In the car park at the Saddleworth Museum and Art Gallery, which is on the A670, the main road through Uppermill.
- **LENGTH OF WALK:** 4¼ miles. Map: OS OL1 Dark Peak Area (GR 996055).

11

After following the route through Uppermill you walk along the Pennine Bridleway and then the Tame Valley Way before descending to the Huddersfield Narrow Canal. The remainder of the walk stays beside this waterway as you head back into Uppermill with its fascinating past – it is an old mill town where once cotton and wool were produced. The museum houses an exhibition of these former days, and the building is itself part of the 19th-century Victoria Mill.

Just before you get back to your car at the museum you will pass, on your right, the licensed café bar that is Jonathan's @ Eutopia. They provide very tasty dishes, 'light bites', during the day which could best be described as mixed Mediterranean-style cuisine – paninis and salads. The food is cooked fresh so you may have a 15 to 20 minute wait, perhaps longer at peak times. In the evenings the dishes get a little 'meatier', such as supreme fillet of halibut with black pepper, lime and tarragon or dry aged fillet of beef with a gorgonzola crust, Portobello mushrooms and red wine gravy. Please note that Jonathan's does not open on Monday or Tuesday. However, there are many other pubs and tearooms in Uppermill, one of the best pubs being the Royal George Hotel which is passed at point 3 of the walk.

Telephone: 01457 876976.

THE WALK

1. Turn left along the main road (the A670) and cross the river. Turn right along Court Street. On reaching the Civic Hall bear left into Lee Street. Turn right at the crossroads with the parish centre on your right. Then turn right for Saddleworth Pool, but almost immediately fork left up steps to the Pennine Bridleway.

2. Turn right along this, signed 'Greenfield ¾'. Keep forward at the car park beside a gravel football pitch on your right. Pass under a bridge lined with corrugated sheeting. Stay on the gravel bridleway beyond. This stretch is surprisingly rural. Go through a gate declaring you are in Higher Arthurs. The bridleway bears right downhill. Turn left along Carr Lane for 20 yards. Bear slightly left to take a path leading back to the Pennine Bridleway (PBW). You then cross a road and keep forward (a signpost should point towards Carrbrook 2½ miles away). Keep forward at another quiet, road keeping to the right of the driveway for Tame Court House. Keep forward along the track at the end of the cul de sac and cross the river Tame, bearing right beyond it. Ignore a path to the right and ascend the wider bridleway ahead of you. The bridleway levels

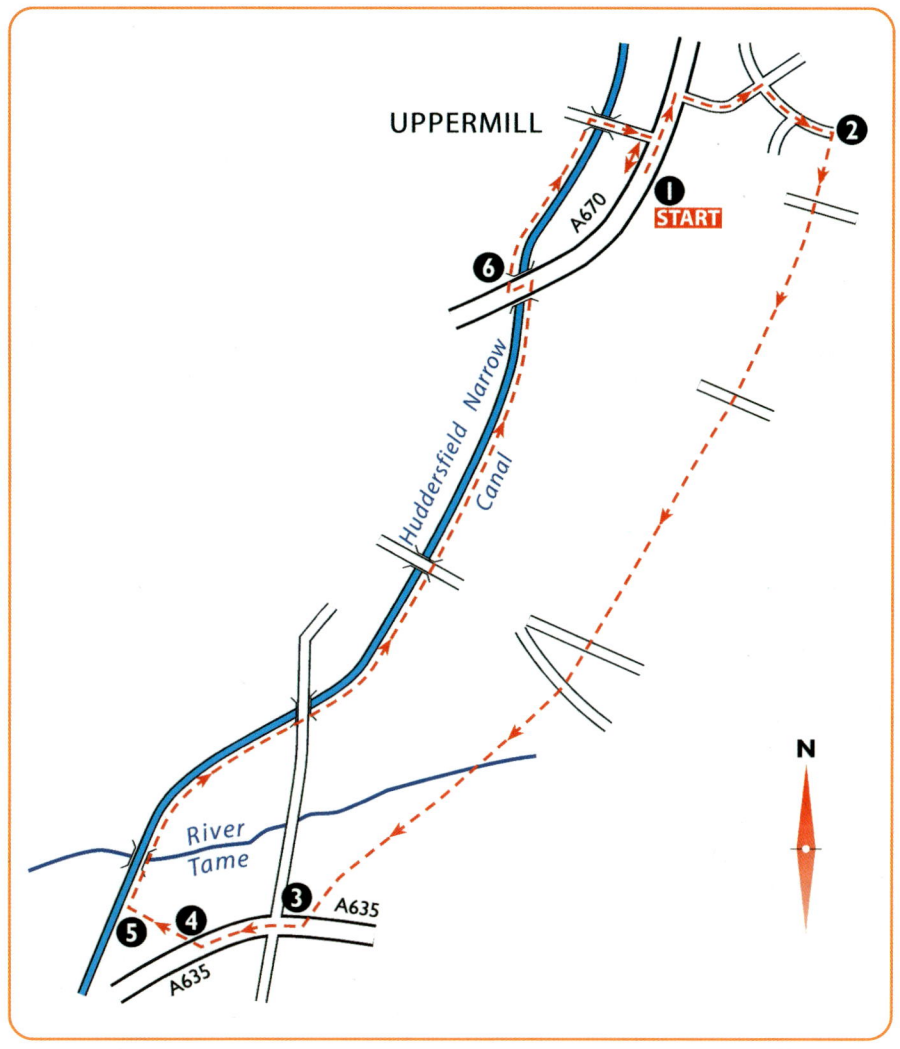

out. Turn right along the Tame Valley Way, leaving the Pennine Bridleway. The hill to the right, with the mast, is Wharmton. Stay on the Tame Valley Way. Pass a car park on your left. The 'Way' then forks, but only for a few yards as the forks soon come back together. You then reach Manchester Road.

3. Keep straight across at the crossroads, passing the Royal George on your left. Proceed down the main road.

The Huddersfield Narrow Canal at Uppermill

4. Just beyond Toll House, No 62, on your right, turn right down a track which is signposted 'Quick'! The track leads down to the canal (ignore the turn for Saddleworth Tennis Club to the right as you go). Walk down to the Huddersfield Narrow Canal. The canal is about 20 miles long and has over 70 locks.

5. Turn right alongside the canal on your left. The canal crosses the river Tame via an aqueduct. Pass under Bridge 83 and rise up to a lock. Then pass under bridges 82, 81 and 80. You then reach Bridge 79 and have to cross it as you can't go underneath. Lock 20W is reached. Keep forward, still with the canal on your left. At Bridge 78, High Street Bridge, rise up the side of it and cross the road (Oldham Road).

6. Continue alongside the canal, now with it on your right. Climb up to Bridge 77, cross it and walk down to the main road (the A670). Turn right back to your car.

PLACES OF INTEREST NEARBY
Do look around the **Saddleworth Museum** and learn something about life hereabouts in days gone by. Telephone: 01457 874093.

At weekends you may even fancy a one-hour boat trip from just beside the car park. Telephone: 0161 6526331 for details.

CROWDEN AND WOODHEAD RESERVOIR

An exhilarating and quite testing walk with tremendous views, climbing high above Woodhead Reservoir and returning along the valley beside the reservoir and the river Etherow.

Descending towards Woodhead

- **HOW TO GET THERE:** Crowden is on the A628 to the north of Glossop. It is approximately 4 miles north-east of Tintwistle.
- **PARKING:** Crowden car park on the northern side of the A628.
- **LENGTH OF WALK:** 6¾ miles. Map: OS OL1 Dark Peak Area (GR 072992).

The scenery is marvellous on this walk but do try and choose the right day. This can be quite a bleak and exposed area in the wrong weather so be prepared and check the forecast before you go out. Initially, you follow the Northern Horse Route, a concessionary bridleway which enables users to avoid the busy main road below. You soon start to rise well above Woodhead Reservoir below and then, before you know it, you are zigzagging downhill into the valley to the river Etherow and a much less exposed return along the Trans Pennine Trail and Longdendale Trail, which follows the route of the old Manchester to Sheffield railway line. This is a toughish walk in the early stages, so don't try it until you know your capabilities.

In Tintwistle look out for the signs for the Bull's Head, on Old Road, and pay it a visit. It's an old pub where both Dick Turpin and John Hatfield, 'The Famous Seducer', were known to partake of liquid refreshment, amongst other things presumably; both of them coming to a sticky end, of course. Then there's the list of landlords dating back to Robert Newton in 1593. It's a pub to be relished, rather like the food and drink. Bombardier beer is usually available plus a guest such as Jennings Cumberland Ale. The food is good wholesome pub food, the sort you want after a walk of nearly 7 miles – Cumberland sausage, bully beef hotpot and home-made cheese and onion pie for example. The George is open all day at the weekend but only in the evening during the week.

Telephone: 01457 853365.

Alternatively, there is the Peels Arms which is less than a mile away in Padfield. Telephone: 01457 852719.

THE WALK

1. From the car park return to the road (the A628). Turn left and in 50 yards enter the wood on your left via the bridlegate or stile. Follow the path through the wood, parallel to the road on the right. The path bears left at the top of the wood. Cross the small bridge over a watercourse before bearing right beyond a gate. The 'NHR' sign represents the Northern Horse Route. The path brings you to a gate. Go through and follow the path down towards the road before swinging left to walk beside it. Leave the open ground by a small gate. Follow the lane (again signed 'NHR') towards a church.

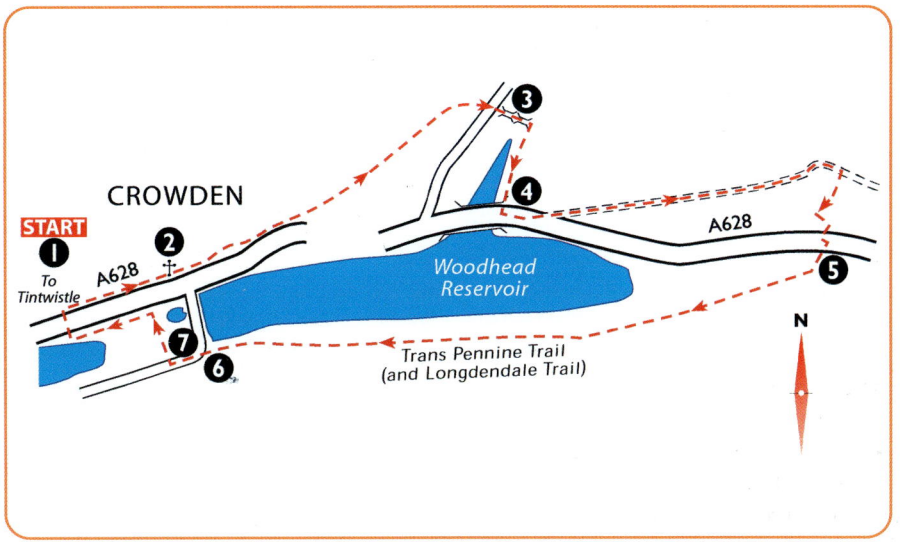

2. On reaching St James' church, have a look around the graveyard: here are the graves of some of the navvies who were killed whilst working on the Woodhead tunnel. The church is, unfortunately, usually closed. Continue along the tarmac and pass through a gate. Follow the grassy track beyond. This takes you high above the western end of Woodhead Reservoir. On reaching a pair of gates, go through the right-hand one. Ignore a double-gate on your left. Follow the track steadily downhill. On reaching the road rise up on a grassy path away from the road. You then cross the hillside staying, basically, on the same level. Eventually you pass through a bridlegate and proceed alongside a plantation on your right. Then go through another bridlegate, keeping forward beside a fence on the left. Proceed until the Northern Horse Route leads you to a lane.

3. Cross the lane. Follow the Northern Horse Route for Woodhead. It clearly drops downhill to cross a substantial bridge. Cross another bridge and turn right with Woodhead Reservoir on your right. Near the road cross a bridge to reach a track.

4. Follow the narrow tarmac lane uphill with the main road to your right. On reaching a stone outbuilding keep forward through a gate (ignoring the private drive to your left). Proceed up the walled green lane. Pass a mast on your right. By an old small quarry pass through a

17

The Woodhead viaduct

gate, still rising uphill, on the green lane with no walls on either side. The track levels out. Ignore a track forking left. The track you are on subsequently swings left and downwards and then right and upwards. Turn right then along the Trans Pennine Trail (signed 'TPT West' and 'Woodhead Tunnel'). Woodhead Reservoir will be ahead of you. The Trail descends steeply back towards the A628. Zigzag down to the road and cross it carefully. Follow the 'TPT West' sign for Torside, 3 miles away.

5. On reaching a car park, go through the gate to follow the Trail. Don't cross the bridge! Keep the watercourse (the river Etherow) on your left. You reach the entrance to the Woodhead Tunnel, which is 3 miles long and opened in 1845 with one railway line. A second line opened in 1852. There was 'much misery and loss of life' amongst the 1,500 navvies who worked here. A large tunnel replaced the smaller ones in 1954 before the railway closed in 1981. Follow the Trail for 1½ miles. The Trans Pennine Trail runs from Hull to Liverpool, 150 miles away.

6. At the end of the reservoir, climb the banking to reach a road. Keep forward, following the Trail beyond. As you go the road will be to your right, and after 100 yards fork right between the Trail and the road, for Crowden.

7. Cross the road and follow the concessionary path away from it. This leads to a pool. Cross the footbridge, descend some steps at the far side and proceed beside a watercourse on your right. Ignore a path crossing the small bridge on your right and keep forward. Pass through a kissing gate and turn right to the road. Turn right along the road, then left back to the car.

PLACES OF INTEREST NEARBY

Not so far away is **Hadfield**, where The League of Gentlemen was filmed for TV. You might like to see if you recognise bits of 'Royston Vasey'!

A bit further afield, just over 10 miles away is **Castleton** with its caverns and mines, and also **Peveril Castle**, the oldest castle in the Peaks.

MORE HALL AND BROOMHEAD RESERVOIRS

A lovely, level walk around More Hall and Broomhead reservoirs to the north of Sheffield. I never realised the Peak Park went this far !

Looking towards More Hall Reservoir

- **HOW TO GET THERE:** Follow the A6102 northwards from Sheffield. Take the left turn for Bolsterstone but instead of following the road to this village take the road to the left of the Bolsterstone road for South Yorkshire Sailing Club (also signed 'More Hall').
- **PARKING:** Park near the dam wall of More Hall Reservoir after ½ mile.
- **LENGTH OF WALK:** 5 miles. Map: OS OL1 Dark Peak Area (GR 287958).

More Hall and Broomhead reservoirs are quite new compared to others in the Peak District, being constructed in the 1930s. They can hold between them approximately 1,500 million gallons of water. Yorkshire Water has recently created some permissive paths which open up the area and you won't be disappointed walking in this lovely wooded valley.

You won't be disappointed with the Castle Inn at Bolsterstone, either. To get there return to the A6102, turn sharp left, and a couple of miles later turn right into the village. The Castle is very popular so get there in good time. During the week food is available from 12 noon until 2 pm and then from 5 pm until 8 pm; at weekends, from 12 noon until 8 pm on Saturday and 4 pm on Sunday. There is plenty of choice for food with the 'Sizzlers' sounding very tasty, whether made with jumbo sausages, a half chicken or lamb chops. There are usually specials such as Cajun chicken or marinated rump steak available too. The vegetarians amongst us will be relieved that they are catered for with dishes like leek and stilton mushrooms. There are usually a couple of guest beers on offer, with Stones Bitter being the regular beer. The pub is home to ('headquarters of', perhaps) the world famous Bolsterstone Male Voice Choir and some of their trophies are on display.

Telephone: 0114 2886300.

THE WALK

1. From the eastern end of More Hall Reservoir walk along the road with the reservoir on your left. In 1 mile you reach another lane at a

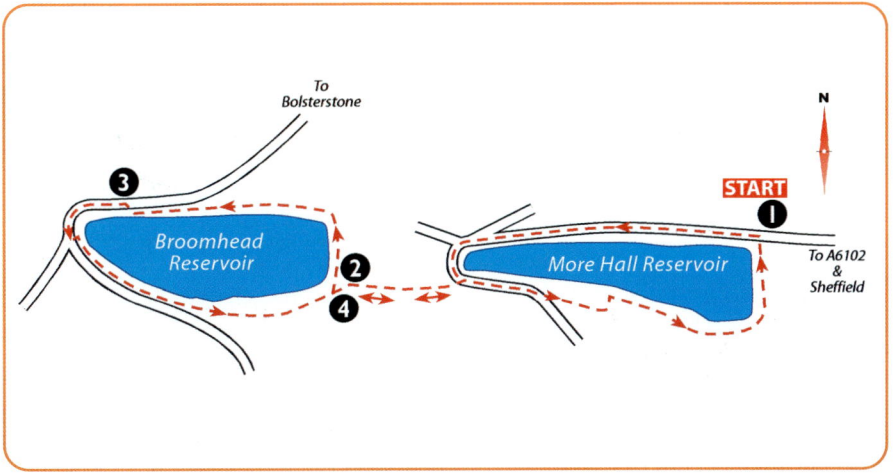

Walking beside More Hall Reservoir

crossroads. Keep left here, passing the Old Sawmill to your right. Where the road bears left take the bridleway leading into Horse Wood. Follow this, rising higher as you walk through the trees. This brings you to the Broomhead Reservoir wall.

2. Turn right across the wall. The houses at the top of the hill are in Bolsterstone. The small gate to get out on to the far side of the wall at the end of the dam is just beyond the large metal gate. Turn left along a permissive path to walk beside the path above the overflow. Follow this for just under 1 mile – it's a bit rougher than before. Ignore any paths to the right.

3. On reaching a lane turn left, there's a bend in the road here so take care, and cross the bridge. Turn left just beyond the bridge into Yorkshire

Water's property. You will be walking between the lane on your right and the reservoir on the left. A section of duckboarding is negotiated. Eventually, ⅔ mile after taking this path, you reach a layby. Bear left here along the wider path through the trees. Ignore a couple of paths to your right which presumably lead back to the lane, some distance away by now.

4. You then come back to the dam wall of Broomhead Reservoir and retrace your steps to descend the bridleway through the wood. On joining the road you left earlier, turn right. Stay on this, passing Jack-House. Just round the corner beyond this, follow the footpath on your left into Morehall Reservoir Plantation. When the path bears right uphill, turn left towards the reservoir. At the waterside turn right. Continue until you reach the sailing club premises, taking the track behind the buildings. Keep on along this and turn left to cross the dam wall back to your car.

PLACE OF INTEREST NEARBY
A stroll around **Bolsterstone**, one of the last hill villages surviving around Sheffield, would be the first suggestion as there are one or two particularly interesting features such as the church, Porter's Lodge and Castle Cottage – the Earls of Shrewsbury once had a manor house here.

LADYBOWER RESERVOIR

Stunning and impressive Peak scenery abounds on this route. How could anyone not enjoy a walk in this area? There is a stretch of steepish walking to get you onto the tops but it's well worth it for the views over the beautiful Ladybower and Derwent reservoirs.

Ladybower Reservoir

- **HOW TO GET THERE:** From the A57 Snake Road, just west of the point where it is joined by the A6013 at Ladybower, drive northwards beside the reservoir, signposted 'Derwent Valley'.
- **PARKING:** Fairholmes car park, after 2½ miles. It can be very busy at weekends and bank holidays.
- **LENGTH OF WALK:** 4¾ miles. Map: OS OL1 Dark Peak Area (GR 172894).

There is so much history on this walk and you will find it commemorated on the route! Whether it's the amazing story of Tip the dog – who stayed with his master's body in the snow for 15 days in 1953 – or the bravery of the Dambusters in the Second World War, you can't help but be impressed. While you're at it, remember the brave men who built the three Derwent dams at the beginning of the 20th century. These navvies lived at Birchinlee (or Tin Town) a little further north of the route of the walk, beside Derwent Reservoir, with their wives and children for over ten years – all 2,500 of them.

To visit the Famous Yorkshire Bridge Inn head back down to the A57, turn left and then right on the A6013. The Inn will be seen just beyond the wall of Ladybower Reservoir. They have accommodation here if you fancy making a weekend of it. There is a comprehensive menu with something to suit everyone (I can certainly recommend the Cheddar cheese and onion toasted sandwich if you're wanting something light). If you're not, then how about a submarine sandwich filled with home-cooked beef or ham; or Moroccan lamb tagine. Then you could order a 'Bit on the Side'. Don't worry, it's just onion rings, mushrooms or a side salad! Excellent beers too, such as Old Peculier, Black Sheep Bitter and Copper Dragon's Challenger IPA.

Telephone: 01433 651361; www.yorkshire-bridge.co.uk.

THE WALK

1. From Fairholmes car park return to the mini roundabout nearby. Take the road which rises uphill (and which at weekends and bank holidays is closed to vehicles, except for access) through a conifer plantation. Do not follow the road turning sharp right which leads you below the wall of Derwent Reservoir. The route you follow should bring you level with this dam wall. Further along, ignore a path sharp left signed 'Fairholmes via Old Railway'. A plaque inside the tower of the dam wall commemorates the night of 16/17 May 1943 when 19 Lancaster bombers of 617 Squadron attacked the Ruhr dams at low level. The 'bouncing bomb' was devised by Dr. Barnes Wallis – a Derbyshire man – and Derwent Dam was chosen for low level flying practice beforehand because of its close resemblance to the German dams; this famous RAF operation was of course filmed as *The Dam Busters*. Also remembered are the 204 air crew of the squadron who laid down their lives between 1943 and 1945. Reach and pass Gores Farm House, staying on the tarmac road beyond.

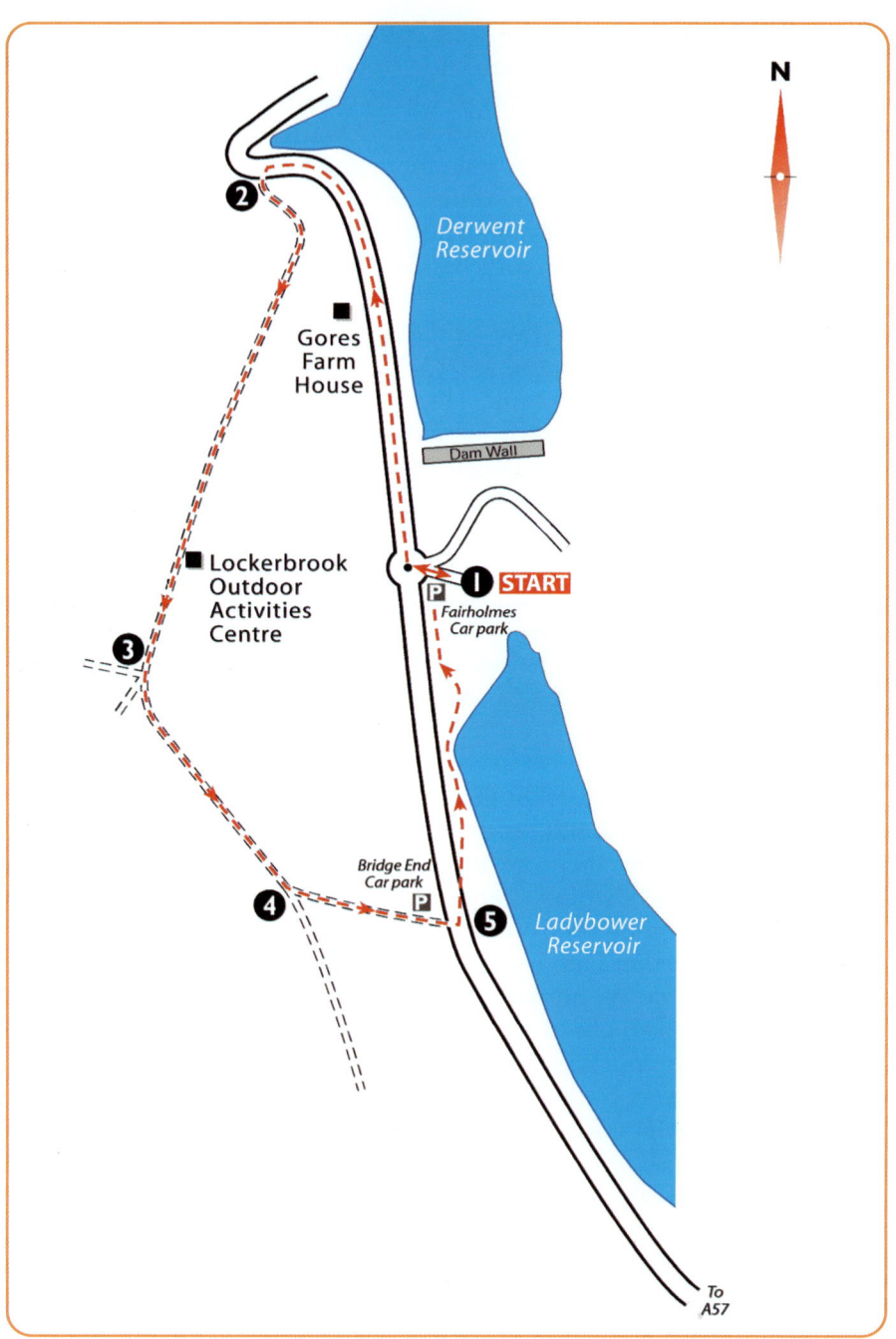

N

Derwent
Reservoir

2

Gores
Farm
House

Dam Wall

Lockerbrook
Outdoor
Activities
Centre

3

1 START

Fairholmes
Car park

Bridge End
Car park

4

5

Ladybower
Reservoir

To
A57

Derwent Reservoir

2. As the road swings left, with an inlet below on your right, there are good views looking up the dam to the wall of Howden Reservoir. Before the road swings sharp right, 600 yards beyond Gores Farm House, there is a gate on your left with a track leading uphill beyond it. Follow this bridleway into the Forestry Commission woodland. There is, quite soon, a sharp left turn which leads you steadily uphill. The bridleway levels out gently. You eventually come out into the open. Ignore a couple of routes to the left leading back downhill to Fairholmes. Keep forward on the track to reach Lockerbrook Outdoor Activities Centre, staying on the track beyond it.

3. After 400 yards the track splits. Ignore the path into the wood on your left to walk beside the plantation on the left for a few yards and then turn left along a bridleway, keeping the trees on the left. Proceed along the ridge for over ½ mile.

4. Fork left downhill through the trees for another ½ mile or so. It is steepish to begin with but then levels out with good views.

5. At the road turn left to reach Bridge End car park on your left. At the end of the car park bear right to pick up the path beside Ladybower Reservoir. Follow this until you rise back up to the road again. Here bear right along the road to come back to Fairholmes.

PLACES OF INTEREST NEARBY

Three miles away, in **Castleton**, are caverns to explore such as **Treak Cliff** (Telephone: 01433 620571) and **Speedwell** (Telephone: 01433 620512). Also in Castleton is the 11th-century **Peveril Castle**. Or you could go and do some more exploring of the beautiful country around the dams by hiring a bike from **Fairholmes**, where you'll probably have parked. From March to October you should be able to hire a bike every day, assuming they're not all being used. At other times you can only hire at weekends, though in December they may be closed. Telephone: 01433 651261.

THE RIVELIN VALLEY

The lovely Rivelin valley is an old industrial area, once full of watermills, and though now woodland growth hides a lot of what was once there, a walk beside the river Rivelin can always reveal something surprising.

The view over the Rivelin Valley

- **HOW TO GET THERE:** This walks starts on the western side of Sheffield. Follow the A57 eastwards from the Peak District towards Sheffield.
- **PARKING:** Shortly after the junction with the A6101 turn left into the car park on Rails Road.
- **LENGTH OF WALK:** 4¼ miles. Map: OS OL1 Dark Peak Area (GR 291872).

Unless you already know the Rivelin valley you will be quite amazed by the beauty of this place. The first stretch of the walk rises up from the car park away from the valley, with views over the countryside. Then you descend to river level again and the rest of the walk involves you walking upstream taking it all in. Take your camera!

I really like the Three Merry Lads. To get there, turn right out of the car park and right on the A57. Then turn left almost immediately. Continue until you reach a crossroads and turn right. The Three Merry Lads is along here on the right. It always seems a friendly, lively pub and the food and beer (such as Abbot Ale, Kelham Island Easy Rider, Tetley Cask and Marstons Pedigree) are great. Foodwise, you could try one of their 'grazing boards' ('great to share'), comprising four meats or Yorkshire cheeses. Then there are the main courses like chef's curry of the day with naan bread and rice, salmon fillet with basil pesto, or try spiced nut paella. There are smaller meals too; great food, great beer, great pub. They open at 11.30 am Monday to Saturday and from 12 noon on Sunday until 3 pm during the week, and all day at the weekend. During the week, of course, they open again in the evening.

Telephone: 0114 2302824.

THE WALK

1. Turn right from the car park entrance. A few yards later, turn left. Follow the gravel path with the river Rivelin on your right. Descend into the trees. Almost immediately fork right across the packhorse bridge. Bear left with the river on the left. The bridleway begins to rise. Ignore a footpath on your left as the track rises a little more steeply, bearing right at the same time. Follow the bridleway up to the A57.

2. Cross this carefully and bear left for 25 yards. Turn right up the public byway and follow this, ignoring paths and a bridleway off it. The byway rises diagonally across the hillside. You reach 'civilisation', but 15 yards before you get to a tarmac road, turn sharp left and drop downhill. Then 20 yards later swing right and follow a narrow path with a drop on your left and a house on the right. Stay on this path to descend some wooden steps. You then keep on it to reach the A57 again.

3. Cross the road and turn right. In 200 yards, on the right-hand bend, turn left off the road, then immediately right along a footpath (ignoring the one to the left). The path runs along the backs of houses. At the end of the wall on your right, at a crossroads of paths, turn sharp left

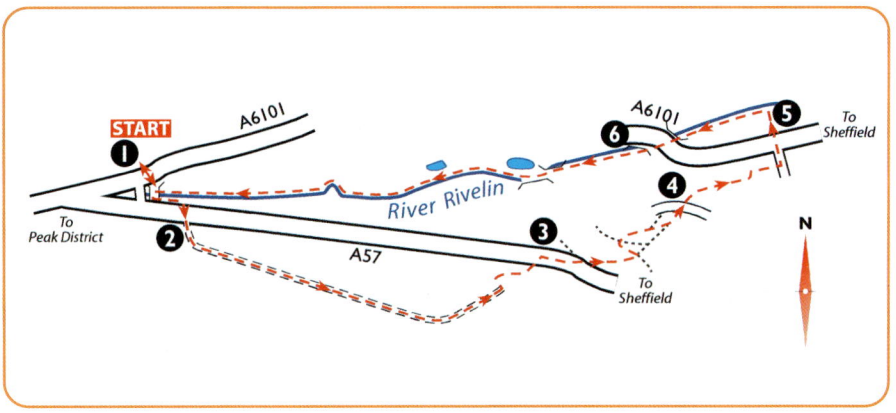

downhill. Subsequently swing sharp right, still descending. Proceed with a wall on your left, ignoring a path dropping downhill from the right that crosses the path you are on. Keeping the wall on your left, proceed for 175 yards, forking right when the bridleway splits. When a path joins yours from a stile at the top of a grassy bank on the right, keep forward in the same general direction as before to reach a lane.

4. Cross the lane, taking the path opposite. Where the path forks inside the wood, ignore the left fork, keeping forward into the field. Keep forward at the same level through the fields. Head to the far end of the fields, losing a little height, walking alongside a small wood on your right. Climb a stile and bear left downhill beside a wall on your left. The bridleway swings right to reach a lane dropping downhill to the left. Descend to the A6101.

5. Cross this and descend the path opposite. On reaching the river, turn left. Walk upstream and remember that in the unlikely event you get lost, just keep walking up the valley. Stay beside the river on your right. Ignore all paths to left and right. Cross a concrete bridge. With the A6101 nearby you reach an open gravel area. Keep forward to pass a dam on your right. Rise up to the main road. Follow this to the right. Half way across the bridge, cross to a path that descends some steps with the river still on the right. The A6101 should be on your right too.

6. You will soon be walking between the river on the right and a shallower man-made watercourse on your left. You reach a fairly solid footbridge with a dam 20 yards beyond. Cross the bridge and walk round

31

In the Rivelin Valley

the dam to your left. The river should now be on your left. On the far side of the dam cross the second footbridge, keeping beside the river on the left. You reach a crossroads of paths, with the path to your left entering a field. Keep forward, climb some steps and walk alongside another dam on your right. Beyond this keep forward to reach another crossroads of paths. Keep forward again with the river still on your left. This brings you into the open. Keep forward and when the path forks, take the left fork. Cross some stepping stones where a stream enters the river and 5 yards later ignore a wooden plank bridge on your left and walk up the steps in front of you. Turn left at the top of the steps (the road is now not very far away). Keep left to get back to the riverside. Follow the path upstream with the river on the left. Where the path forks, take the lower fork which will bring you back to the packhorse bridge so that you can follow your way back to your car.

PLACES OF INTEREST NEARBY
Can I do any better than suggest you visit Sheffield? There's **Graves Art Gallery** (telephone 0114 2782600), the **Botanical Gardens** (telephone 0114 2500500) and the **Peace Gardens**, to name but a few of the city's attractions.

LYME PARK AND THE MACCLESFIELD CANAL

A wonderful walk on the western side of the Peak District with no particularly steep climbs or descents. There's a marvellous mix of rolling countryside and canalside walking, plus beautiful Lyme Park to enjoy.

The Macclesfield Canal

- **HOW TO GET THERE:** Follow the A6 for 12 miles north of Buxton, turning left into Lyme Park.
- **PARKING:** In 1½ miles park in the large car park with the Hall to your left. A fee is payable unless you are a National Trust member.
- **LENGTH OF THE WALK:** 5½ miles. Map: OS OL1 Dark Peak Area (GR 963824).

After slowly descending along a track out of the National Trust property, Lyme Park, there then follows 1½ miles beside the Macclesfield Canal where there is always something to see. Not only are there all sorts of narrow boats, but when I walked here in September I saw a swallow skimming the water, starlings eating the hawthorn berries, Canada geese grazing on the far side and 20 or more goldfinches feeding on thistle seeds. The return features the rather lovely hedged Cow Lane before a stretch along a quietish lane brings you back into Lyme Park and the enjoyable last section of walking beneath some of the trees in the park.

There are two options if you want something to eat. You can either visit the coffee shop in the workshop courtyard for sandwiches and snacks (open from 10.30 am until 5 pm) or if you are wanting something more, try the restaurant in the Hall itself. Here the dishes are rather more substantial so you might like to try Lyme venison or pan-fried breast of Freedom Farm chicken. Lunches are served between 11.30 am and 2.30 pm, before afternoon teas from 2.30 pm until 5 pm. Both eating establishments are likely to be closed midweek during the winter.
  Telephone: 01663 762023.

THE WALK

1. Turn left along the road between the car park and the pond. Keep on it as it swings right, passing through a gate by a cattle grid. (Ignore the path to the left at this point.) The road you are on rises up an incline. Subsequently bear right along a rough track towards a wall. When the track forks again, go right so you are walking beside the wall on your right. Keep down the track to pass through a tall kissing gate by a house. Proceed down the track beyond, passing Haresteads Farm. Keep on, ignoring another track sharp right signed 'Hilltop Farm'.

2. You will eventually arrive at the Macclesfield Canal. Cross Bridge 15 and keep right to pass under it. Walk alongside the canal on your left and enjoy the colourful scene. You reach a stone milestone on your right with the place-names obliterated – perhaps this was done during World War II just in case we were invaded. Pass under Bridge 16. On the right just beyond it there is a lovely memorial to Harold and Betsy Hayes, 'together at last'. Pass under Bridge 17 and enjoy a delightful stretch of canalside walking. You pass Lyme View Marina across on the other side of the canal and then reach Bridge 18.

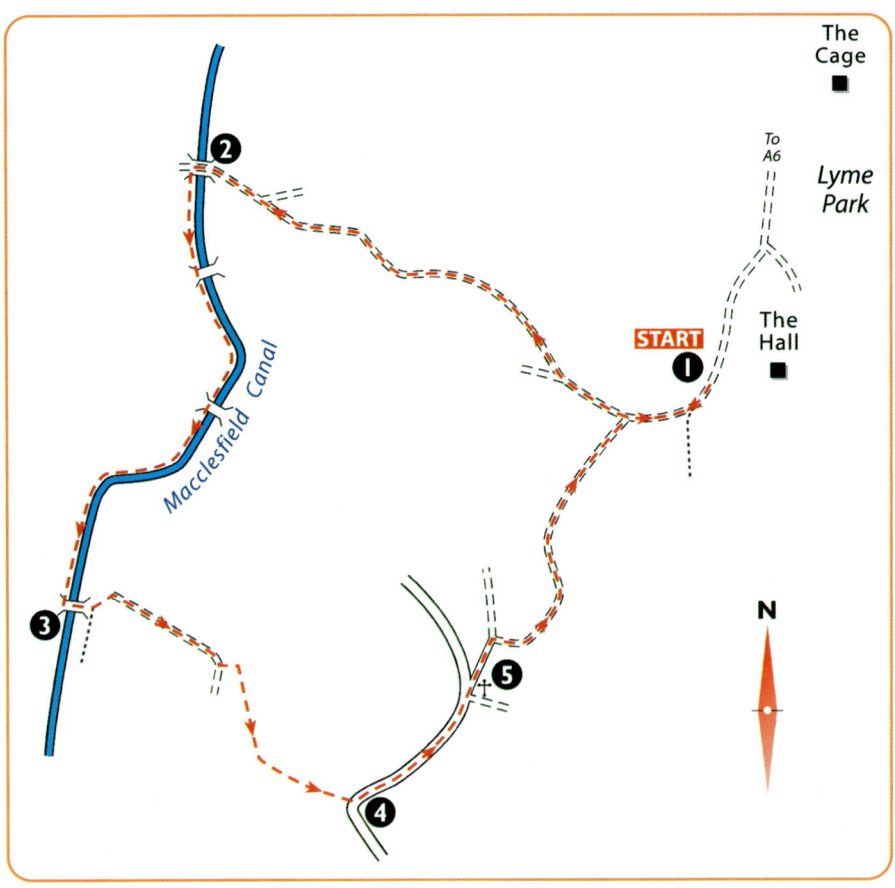

3. Cross this bridge, leaving the canal. Once beyond the bridge ignore a path to your right but turn right up the 'private road' for Lockgate Farm. Keep along this track. Half-left The Cage (an 18th-century hunting tower) may be visible 2 miles away. Where the driveway bears right into the stud farm, keep forward, climbing a stile to head across the paddock to cross another stile. Then turn right to climb another stile a few yards away. Bear slightly left beyond this to cross the field ahead. On the far side of the field turn left (keeping in the field) and walk up the field with the hedge on your right. This brings you to a gate. Beyond this, walk up the short green lane between hedges. This is known as Cow Lane.

4. When you reach a tarmac lane, turn left for ½ mile, taking care as you go.

Lyme Hall

5. On reaching the Methodist church at Green Close, Pott Shrigley, keep straight forward, leaving the lane you were on. Immediately before West Lodge turn right into Lyme Park. Keep on the stony track through the woodland. This is West Park Drive running through an area called Haze (or Hase) Bank. The National Trust is trying to eradicate the rhododendrons hereabouts. Continue along the track for some way, rising as you go, to reach a gate with a car park beyond. Walk through this and follow the access road. Ignore the gravel track turning sharp left that you used before. Continue back to your car.

PLACES OF INTEREST NEARBY
A visit to **Lyme Hall** itself (open March to October) and its delightful gardens would be the perfect way to end the day. Telephone: 01663 762023.

HATHERSAGE AND THE RIVER DERWENT

This is a super walk beside the river Derwent that uses the beautiful Derwent Valley Heritage Way, a fairly recent addition to the list of long distance paths.

Walking back into Hathersage

- **HOW TO GET THERE:** If you travel from Grindleford on the B6001, the car park on Oddfellows Road is signposted on the right shortly after entering Hathersage.
- **PARKING:** Public car park on Oddfellows Road – get there early as it soon fills up.
- **LENGTH OF WALK:** 6 miles. Map: OS OL1 Dark Peak Area (GR 231814).

The Derwent Valley Heritage Way leads you all the way upstream to the village of Shatton before the walk swings back higher up the hillside. You then descend again to the river before crossing it over stepping stones (assuming the river isn't in flood) and strolling back after a lovely few hours' walk. You will pass by the stepping stones on the outward leg so, if the river is in flood, the options are either to turn around there and then, or continue to point 5 of the walk before returning to the start along the route used earlier. The Way runs from Ladybower beside the river all the way to Derwent Mouth, 55 miles later, south of Derby. It is well served by public transport so it might be a route you could come back to another day, or at least part of it.

If you've driven from Grindleford you will have passed the Plough at Leadmill Bridge – it was on your right just before you entered Hathersage. If you didn't, turn right out of the car park and then left at the main road. The Plough will be on your left after just over ½ mile … and it is well worth visiting. It is open from 11.30 am to 11 pm Monday to Saturday and from 12 noon until 10.30 pm on Sunday. They have several different beers that they take turns in serving, with at least three of them on tap at any one time, so you could perhaps try Timothy Taylor Landlord, Greene King IPA and Fuller's London Pride one day and something different a week later. Foodwise, the Plough caters for everyone whether you want a sandwich, perhaps ham or something more exotic like prawn and avocado in a marie rose sauce, or a more substantial choice such as halibut Lyonnaise with buttered spinach or game torte with fondant potato and red cabbage.

Telephone: 01433 650319.

THE WALK

1. Return to the entrance of the car park and turn right down to the B6001. Turn left for 100 yards. Turn right down Dore Lane. Pass under the railway bridge and continue down the lane. On reaching the entrance to Nether Hall, turn left along the track. Continue alongside a hedge on your right, ignoring the track to the right near the end of the first field which goes to a farm. Proceed along the path in the second field to reach the B6001 again.

2. Turn right to cross Leadmill Bridge and then right immediately beyond to follow the Derwent Valley Heritage Way beside the river. Stay beside the Derwent for the next couple of miles, keeping the river on your right all the time. As you go you will see the stepping stones on

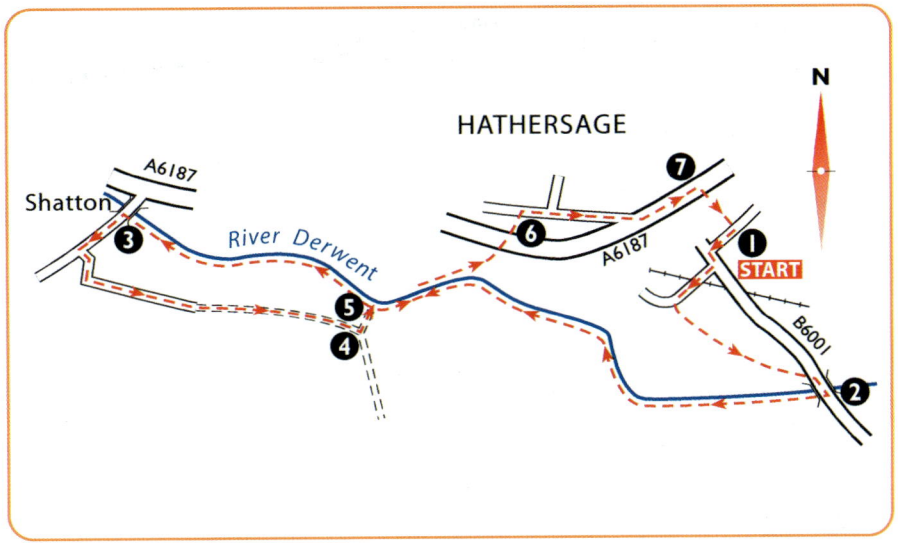

your right leading over to the other side of the river – but don't cross them yet.

3. Eventually you reach the village of Shatton. Turn left up the road and after 400 yards turn sharp left along a lane immediately beyond Greenways (immediately before Brookside). Stay on this lane, ignoring a footpath to your right on a 90 degree left-hand bend. Similarly, ignore the driveway into Westfield. Keep forward through the gateway (signed 'Offerton') when you reach Garner House Farm on your right. The lane has by now become a track.

4. Just over ½ mile later the track bears right steeply uphill towards Offerton Hall and there's also a tarmac track downhill to the left towards some outbuildings. Immediately before this tarmac track though, turn left over a stile and walk down a grassy track parallel to the tarmac track. Follow the grassy track to the river.

5. Turn right alongside the river, following the route you used earlier. On reaching the stepping stones cross these to the far side (or alternatively return to the start from here if the river is in flood). On the other side of the river, turn right with the river on your right. After 500 yards, with the path beneath some electricity lines, leave the riverside and follow the path to the far corner of the field.

The stepping stones across the Derwent

6. Cross the A6187 and climb the stile on the far side. Follow the path, crossing the railway line carefully. Then bear half-right in the field beyond to walk up to the lane. Turn right along the lane and stay on it, ignoring all paths and roads to left and right. The road descends into the centre of Hathersage and you join the main road. Turn left here.

7. In 300 yards, use the pelican crossing to reach the other side of the road. Turn left for a few yards before turning right through the Hathersage Methodist church grounds to return to the car park on the far side.

PLACES OF INTEREST NEARBY

You could head back up to the church in Hathersage and have a look at **Little John's Grave**. Yes, that Little John, Robin Hood's companion. Or drive up to the **Longshaw Estate** and have a stroll around and a cup of tea up there. To get there follow the A6187 towards Sheffield and look out for the signs in the vicinity of Fox House. Telephone: 01433 637904 (Visitor Centre) for further information.

CALVER AND THE RIVER DERWENT

There is so much to enjoy on this walk through some of the Peak District's finest scenery alongside the Derwent. There is one steady and gentle climb, but on the way back you're on the level with lovely riverside walking.

Celandines beneath the trees

- **HOW TO GET THERE:** Travelling northwards along the A623 from Baslow you reach the traffic lights at Calver crossroads. Turn left here as though you're heading for Bakewell. Then turn immediately left into Sough Lane.
- **PARKING:** Park down near the cricket ground where the road is wider.
- **LENGTH OF WALK:** 6¼ miles. Map: OS OL24 White Peak Area (GR 240747).

The walk starts off along Donkey Lane before you climb Hare Knoll. You'll be thinking you are in for an animal-themed walk but alas, it doesn't last, although please let me know if you see the brook lampreys. You climb to the peaceful little village of Curbar with its unusual water trough. Walk this route at the right time of year and marvel at the celandines just south of Curbar. Then you could admire the churchyard in Baslow and the view from the bridge there … and look out for the fish in the small stream at the bottom of the gardens once you're back in Calver.

The Bridge Inn at Calver has Abbot Ale on tap so it's worth going for that alone. But there's more, as the food is always tasty. Beside the items on the menu (such as Cumberland sausage, gammon and egg, and Cajun chicken breast), there's a specials board and vegetarian dishes too. Food is served from 12 noon until 2 pm and from 6.30 pm until 8.30 pm every day though there are no evening meals on Sunday and Monday. To get there, turn right at the end of Donkey Lane and follow the main road down to Baslow; the Bridge Inn is on your left as you go.

Telephone: 01433 630415.

THE WALK

1. With the cricket ground on your left, walk to the end of it and turn left along Donkey Lane. Turn right at the main road, then cross the road shortly afterwards to follow the track uphill. Stay on this as it bears right. After 200 yards, turn sharp left and 125 yards later cross the step-over on your right. This is Hare Knoll and by now you should have great views of Curbar Edge, the outcrop of rock a mile or so away. Walk beside the wall on your left through the first field to reach a ruined building in the second field. Cross the stile and walk down the right side of the third field into the bottom corner. Whilst still in the field, turn left passing through a gateway on your right, 100 yards later. Aim for the stile on the left side of the wall on the opposite side of the field. Descend the path beyond to the road.

2. Cross the road carefully and walk beside the river Derwent for over ½ mile. As you go you cross Stoke Brook by a footbridge and bear right. Look out for the brook lampreys between March and June! Go to http://www.English-nature.org.uk/LifeInUKRivers/species/lamprey.html and have a look at the teeth of a lamprey – you will probably be horrified. It is not unlike an eel but grows to no more than 9 inches. Henry I apparently died of a surfeit of lampreys, although whether brook, river or sea lampreys is unclear.

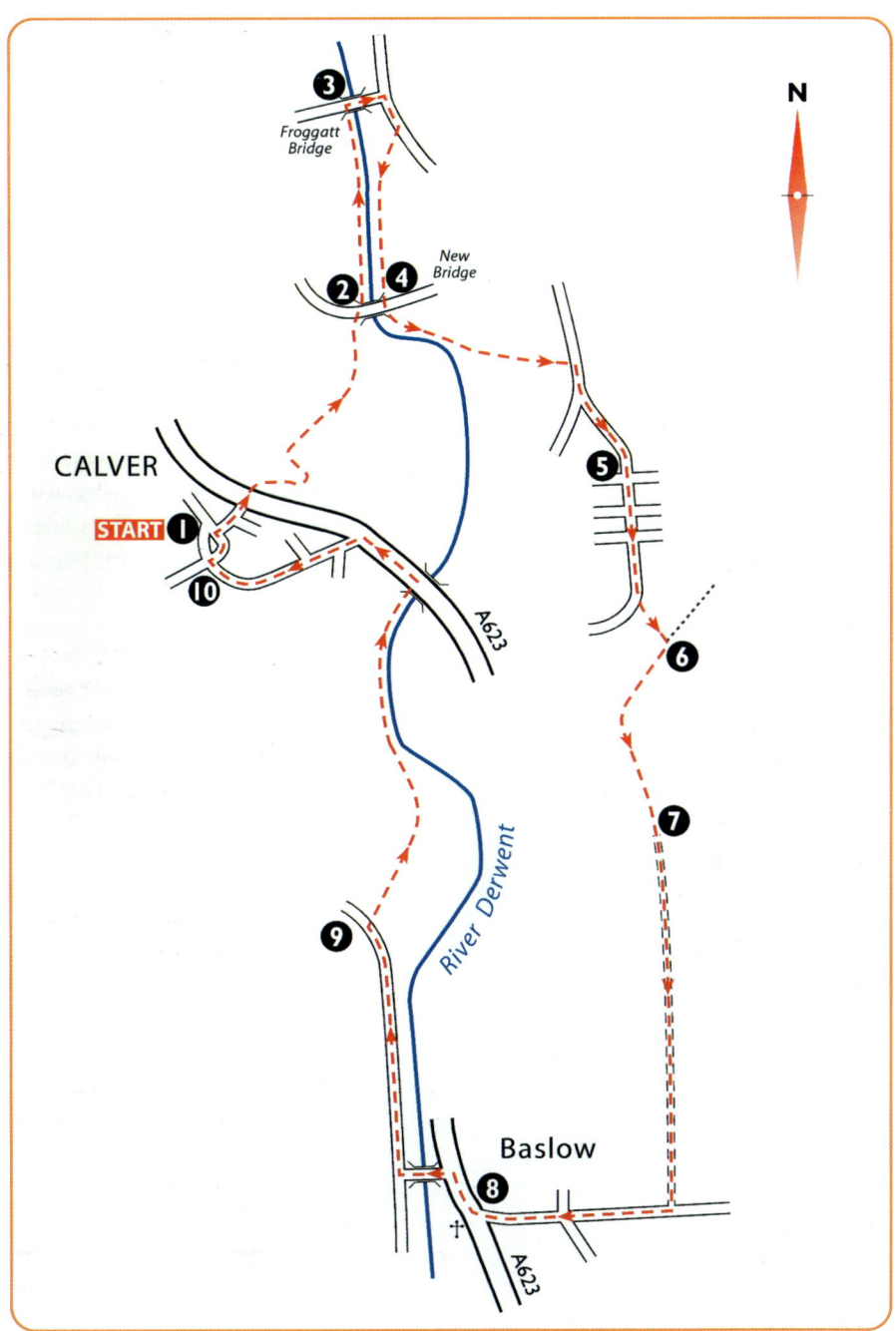

3. On reaching Froggatt Bridge, cross this and keep right. In 75 yards climb a step stile, following the path downstream with the Derwent still on your right.

4. At New Bridge, cross the road and proceed along the path beyond. After 200 yards, just beyond the curved weir, leave the riverside path, forking left, slightly uphill towards a squeezer. Pass through this, walking to the top right corner of the field beyond. Turn right along the lane. Subsequently ignore Dukes Drive to the right (for Calver). Keep forward into the village of Curbar.

5. At the crossroads you might want to take a seat at Spring Well, which when I was last there had a resident frog. Keep forward at the next crossroads along The Hillock. Keep forward at another crossroads to reach Bar Road which runs downhill from left to right. Cross this, walking along Cliff Lane. This bears right. Immediately beyond Curbar Croft climb the steps on your left (signed 'Baslow via Gorse Bank Farm'). Follow the path between wall and hedge. Then walk down the right side of a paddock to reach a walled path.

6. Turn right beside a tiny stream. Go through a wicket gate, following a paved path and passing through another small gate. Aim for the property at the top of the rise, walking beside a wall on your right. Pass

View of the Derwent from the bridge in Baslow

through another gate to rise up to a gate to the left of the property. Then bear right to a gate 20 yards later, keeping forward in the field beyond that. Descend gently to walk down the right side of a rocky field. Turn left beyond a squeezer stile to go through a gate that brings you onto a fenced path leading to Gorse Bank Farm, 250 yards away.

7. Walk directly through the farm, continuing along the driveway beyond for ½ mile. On reaching the outskirts of Baslow keep forward to reach a grass triangle and turn right. At a larger grass triangle, bear right down School Lane – keeping the village shop to your right. You reach the church on the far side of the A623.

8. Turn right on the A623, noting the church clock which reads 'VICTORIA 1867'. Turn left beyond the church over the Derwent. Turn right on the far side and proceed along here for ½ mile or so.

9. Some 250 yards beyond Bubnell Farm, follow the footpath on the right to the far corner of the field. Keep forward in the second field to enter a wood. Stay beside the river Derwent on the right until you reach the A623 footbridge. Don't pass under it, but climb the steps immediately before the bridge and walk along the A623. Ignore the first left (Riverside Drive). Take the second left, signed 'Calver village', ignoring the footpath sharp left. Stay on the road, ignoring all roads off it, though just beyond Smithy Knoll Road, walk on the right side of the road and look out for the stream running along the bottom of the gardens. There are even rainbow trout in it. The road rises and then bears right through the village.

10. On reaching the lamp surmounting a stone commemorating Queen Victoria's coronation on 28 June 1838, bear right to follow the lane known as Folds Head. This swings left back to where you left your car.

PLACES OF INTEREST NEARBY

To the west along the A623, after a couple of miles, there is a right turn to **Eyam**, pronounced 'Eem'. It is known as the 'Plague Village' because in 1665 and 1666 its inhabitants were decimated by the bubonic plague. They isolated themselves so as not to spread the disease to neighbouring villages. By the time the plague had burnt itself out over 250 villagers had died. Don't let me spoil the story though. Walk around Eyam and learn a bit more, and do visit Eyam Museum (telephone: 01433 631371).

THE GOYT VALLEY

The scenery on this walk through the Goyt Valley is sublime and there's a seat overlooking Fernilee Reservoir towards the end where you'll want to tarry a while and watch the world go by.

The Goyt Valley

- **HOW TO GET THERE:** Follow the A5004 out of Buxton and 2 miles later, turn left for the Goyt Valley.
- **PARKING:** A mile down the road (at the bottom of a long straight incline) park in the layby on the right-hand side, marked as Bunsal Cob on the OS map). There is alternative parking on the far side of the reservoir too, near Point 4 on the walk.
- **LENGTH OF THE WALK:** 3 miles. Map: OS OL24 White Peak Area (GR 018758).

The first part of the walk is in the open, on what used to be the route of the Cromford and High Peak Railway line linking Cromford with Whaley Bridge, before changing character on the return as you walk below the trees. There's much more to the Goyt Valley than this walk but it gives you a taster of the stunning landscape hereabouts. The Fernilee and Errwood reservoirs were constructed in the first half of the 20th century to provide water for the people of Stockport. It is believed that the remains of a gunpowder factory lie beneath Fernilee Reservoir, which was still in use during the First World War. There are quite a few seats on this short walk so take a flask of coffee with you!

If you travel south from the Goyt Valley along the A6 into Buxton, there are plenty of pubs and tea rooms to choose from. Drive up to Buxton Market Place and search out the 16th-century Old Sun Inn (telephone: 01298 23452) where there's plenty of choice as regards food and beer.

Perhaps you'd prefer to sample some non-alcoholic fare? If so, there are plenty of tea rooms available in the town. If you travel north, you will reach Whaley Bridge where there are plenty of pubs as you head along the A5004. This includes the Cock (telephone: 01663 719341) on the right-hand side.

THE WALK

1. From your car, head along the road towards the reservoirs. The road bears round to the left. Before you reach the dam wall turn sharp right down a tarmac access route. This is signed 'Public Footpath'. It descends towards the side of Fernilee Reservoir. Follow the track beside the reservoir on your left. A mile later at the far end of the reservoir, turn left over the dam wall. On the far side bear left, following a narrow tarmac lane beneath the trees.

2. Immediately before the lane bends sharp right uphill, fork left onto a path leading into the trees. Initially you walk beside a wildlife refuge on your left. This section of the walk is quite different from the first part, being more sheltered. Ignore a grassy track bearing right uphill. Stay on the main path which is largely on the level.

3. On reaching a deepish gulley on your left, fork left on a path leading down towards the reservoir. This zigzags downhill until you get nearer the water. A sign shows you are walking towards Errwood Hall; Deep Clough being uphill to your right. Proceed with the reservoir on your

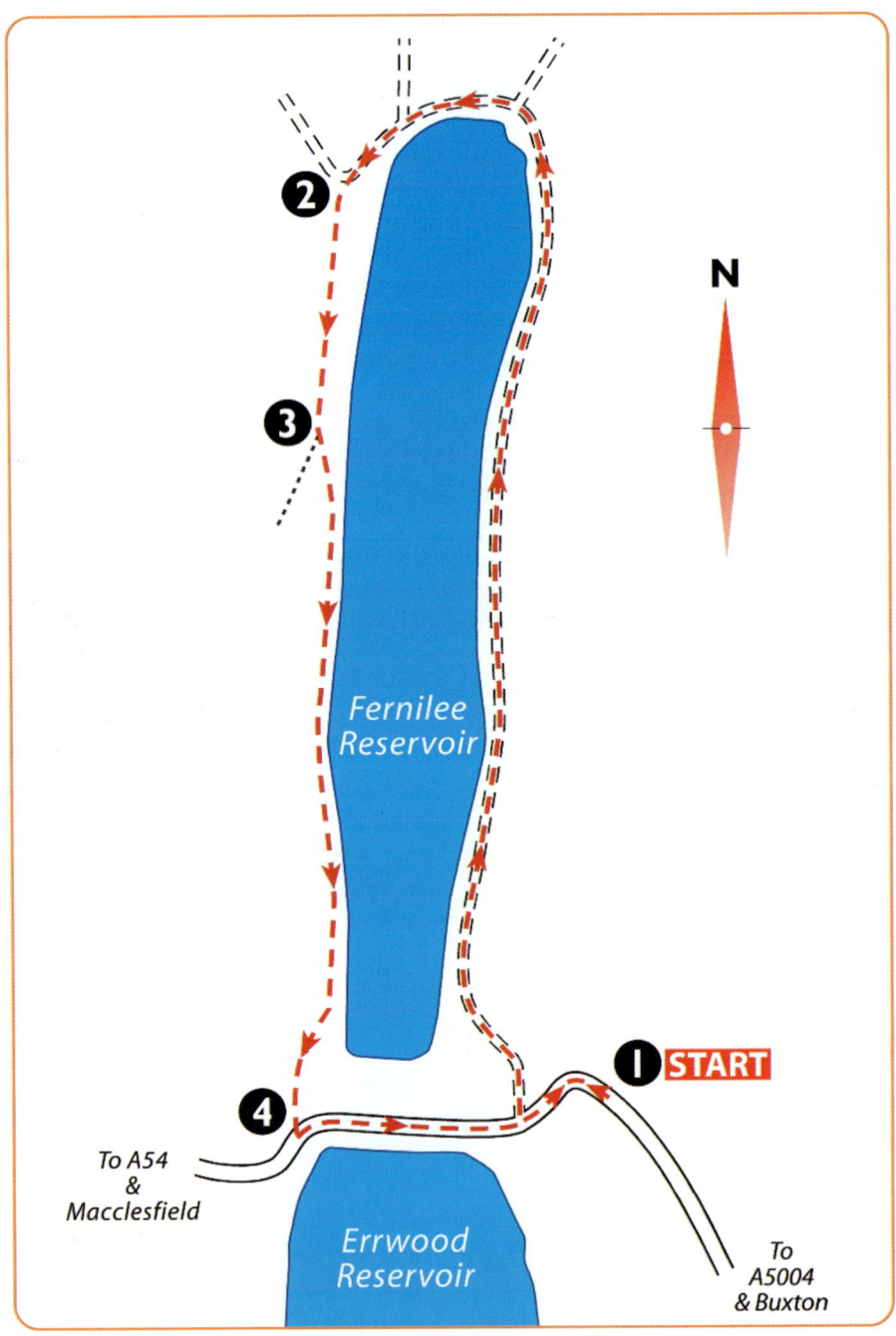

N

2

3

Fernilee Reservoir

1 START

4

To A54 & Macclesfield

Errwood Reservoir

To A5004 & Buxton

left. Towards the end of the reservoir (with the overflow on the far side approximately 100 yards away) fork right uphill on a path signposted 'Errwood'. Keep forward to reach a tarmac lane.

4. Turn left to cross the Errwood Reservoir wall. A plaque commemorates the inauguration of the reservoir on 14 June 1968 by HRH the Duchess of Kent. Walk across the dam wall with the water on your right. Swing left at the far side before bearing right back to your car.

PLACES OF INTEREST NEARBY

One option would be to explore more of the beautiful **Goyt Valley**. Alternatively, head into **Buxton** and have a stroll around the lovely **Pavilion Gardens** (telephone: 01298 23114) or explore the shops. You might want to try the water of St Ann's Well near the Crescent.

Infant pine cones

MACCLESFIELD FOREST AND RESERVOIRS GALORE!

Magical Macclesfield Forest! Winding between four reservoirs before climbing up Hacked Way Lane into the trees, the shafts of sunlight create delightful vistas. And then there's Forest Chapel ... well, you're going to have to follow this delightful walk to see if the magic works for you.

Looking back at Tegg's Nose

- **HOW TO GET THERE:** On the A537 east of Buxton, take the first left ⅔ mile after the Cat and Fiddle. A mile later fork left at the Stanley Arms and after 350 yards fork right. Stay on this road, ignoring another road to the right, to a T-junction. Turn right here to Trentabank Visitor Centre.
- **PARKING:** At Trentabank Visitor Centre. There is some roadside parking too. Get there early!
- **LENGTH OF WALK:** 5 miles. Map: OS OL24 White Peak Area (GR 962711).

This man-made landscape (the first two reservoirs were built in the mid-19th century to provide fresh water for Macclesfield) is well worth exploring and don't forget your binoculars as there's a heronry across the road from the car park. Part of the walk is along the Gritstone Trail, a long distance path that stretches from Lyme Park to Rushton Spencer. Macclesfield Forest was once a royal hunting ground. St Stephen's Chapel has a 1673 date stone over the door but it seems the chapel was rebuilt in 1834.

If you smell the cooking from the Nice Nosh van you may be tempted to try some open air cooking and I wouldn't blame you as there's a tasty selection of dishes, including Povey's Staffordshire oatcakes (telephone: 01298 25930 for more details). Or you could pay a visit to Leathers Smithy, a busy, popular pub (even on the most inhospitable of days, weatherwise) with a friendly welcome and good food. They open all day at the weekend and in the week from 12 noon to 3 pm and from 7 pm to 11 pm; food is available during the day between 12 noon and 2 pm. The menu is varied, from coarse country game terrine to traditional roast beef. The regular beers are Morland Old Speckled Hen, Theakston Best Bitter and Wells Bombardier with guests such as Hydes Atomic. You'll be torn as to where to eat. You'll have to come back!

Telephone: 01260 252313.

THE WALK

1. Walk to the road and turn left downhill. At the junction, bear right and stay on this lane (designated a 'Quiet Lane') as it runs along the northern side of Ridgegate Reservoir.

2. At the end of the reservoir, Leather's Smithy will be in front of you. Turn left along the footpath on the western side of the reservoir. To the right you may get a glimpse of Jodrell Bank. The footpath/track swings left into the plantation – take the path to the right immediately before the trees along the Gritstone Trail. Descend some steps into a wooded valley. Cross a stream by a wooden footbridge and climb up the path to turn right through a wicket gate to reach a track. Turn right and follow this to the road.

3. Turn left, walking along the road with Bottoms Reservoir on your right. After 400 yards, with Redhouse Cottage on your left, turn right along the Gritstone Trail. Keeping Bottoms Reservoir on your right, follow the path round to cross the bridge over the overflow and climb

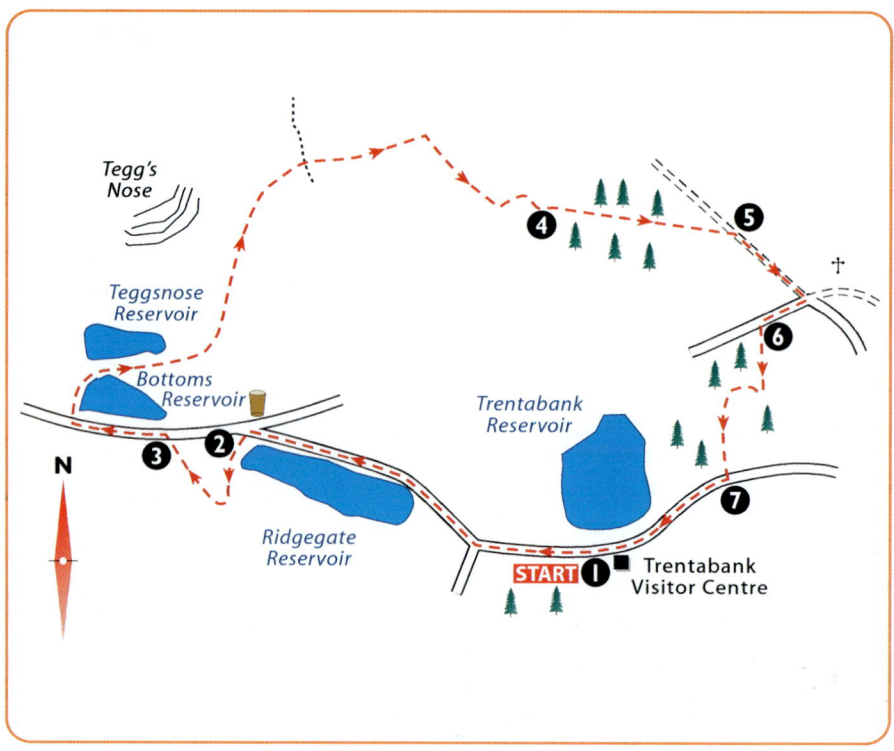

some steps. On joining a narrow lane at the top, turn right. Teggsnose Reservoir is on your left. Stay on the track to enter Tegg's Nose Country Park. The track splits. Take the left fork and drop down to cross a stream. Then keep forward, climbing some wide steps and ignoring narrower ones to the left. Stay on this bridleway to pass Clough House (a farm) below on your right. This brings you to a crossroads. Go straight across for Macclesfield Forest. You descend quite quickly down a tarmac lane, before rising just as quickly. Pass Lower Crooked Yard Farm as the track becomes quite stony. Stay on this as it winds up and down, in and out. It then swings left towards a property (ignore a track to the right at this point). In front of the property, bear right up a tarmac lane. This then bends left and upwards.

4. Almost immediately climb a stile into the wood. Follow the path for Forest Chapel and 200 yards later ignore a path turning sharp left for Walker Barn. Continue until you reach a large stone outbuilding. Just beyond this cross a track and follow the narrow path uphill, signed

In Macclesfield Forest

'Forest Chapel'. This path rises through woodland and in ½ mile you reach Charity Lane.

5. Turn right here, heading downhill on the stony sunken track. At the crossroads 300 yards later turn right along the tarmac road. Before you do, visit the chapel of St Stephen. Back on the route, you reach a footpath on your left after 200 yards.

6. Turn left down this. Ignore a path coming in from the left (from Standing Stone). Continue downhill. On reaching a small pond on your left, turn right for Trentabank. This path becomes a wide-ish track with a deer fence on your left. On reaching a gate, with the wildlife sanctuary beyond, turn left down steps to a lane.

7. Cross this, following the path beyond to the right. The lane is never far from you. Trentabank Reservoir should be visible ahead to your right. In 300 yards after joining this path, pass out onto the road and proceed along it to get a closer look at the fourth of the reservoirs passed today. At the end of the lay-by (from where you can view the Trentabank Heronry) follow the wide path running parallel to the road on your left; 70 yards later pass through a gate on your left and cross the road back to the start.

PLACES OF INTEREST NEARBY

Head west for **Macclesfield** itself and look round the town, famous for the production of silk in years gone by. Or visit **Gawsworth Hall** just south-west of Macclesfield (telephone: 01260 223456).

MILLERS DALE AND THE RIVER WYE

This splendid walk is never more than a good stone's throw from the course of the charming river Wye – full of fish (just keep your eyes open) and wildlife. You might even glimpse a water vole or two.

The disused lime kilns

- **HOW TO GET THERE:** Follow the A6 westwards from the Taddington bypass. Pass the Waterloo pub on your left. After ½ mile turn right on the B6049 and continue down into the valley. After crossing the river Wye, turn left uphill to Millers Dale Station car park.
- **PARKING:** At Millers Dale Car park.
- **LENGTH OF WALK:** 4½ miles. Map: OS OL24 White Peak Area (GR 137732).

The first part of the walk follows the Monsal Trail (the old Midland Railway line) to Litton Mill before the quiet riverside lane brings you back into the village of Millers Dale, once the home of quarrymen and railway workers. Then you have an option: get back in your car, or add another riverside mile or so on to your walk. Go on, you know it makes sense!

The George Hotel can be reached by dropping back down to the B6049 and turning left to follow it up to Tideswell. As you pass through the village look out for the church, the George Hotel is next door. There's plenty of choice on the menu from bar meals of steak and Kimberley Ale pie to Thai chicken; from lasagne verdi to beef madras. There are vegetarian meals too – ratatouille au gratin and mushroom fennel casserole to name but two.

Telephone: 01298 871382.

THE WALK

1. Walk forward towards the old railway line and turn left along the Monsal Trail, signed 'Litton Mill' and 'Bakewell'. A bridge takes you high above the road below. Continue along the Trail passing Millers Dale Quarry – a Site of Special Scientific Interest managed by Derbyshire Wildlife Trust. You also pass the Priestcliffe Lees Reserve, also managed by the Trust. In the trees to your left you may catch a glimpse of Ravenstor Youth Hostel. It was hereabouts that a young David Bellamy became interested in things botanical.

2. A mile after leaving the car, pass under a bridge and fork left on a path for Litton Mill. A footbridge crosses the river Wye and brings you out into Litton Mill itself. To your right is the 19th-century mill which gave this small collection of houses its name; it has recently been converted into luxury apartments. You must turn left though, out of Litton Mill, walking alongside the river on your left. This quiet lane brings you into the small village of Millers Dale – as you go, ignore all footpaths to left and right.

3. After passing the Anglers Rest on your right, continue until you reach the main road, the B6049, just past the remains of the Old Meal Mill (complete with waterwheel in situ). Cross the road and follow the footpath to the left of the church. This zigzags up out of the valley. Pass through a gate into a field and keep up the left-hand side of this. Across the other side of the dale, to your right, is Monksdale Farm. To your left

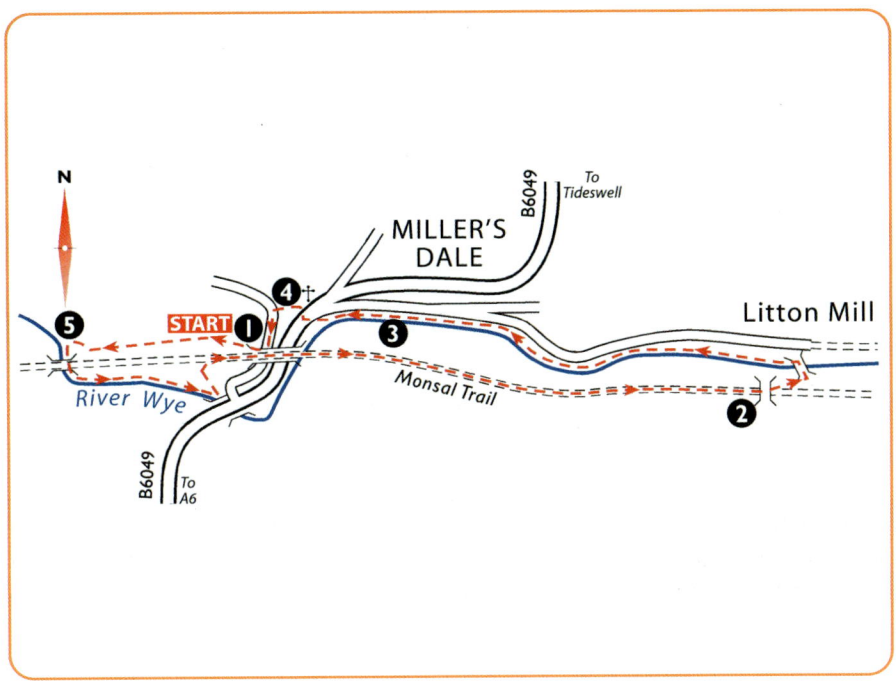

is the Monsal Trail with Millers Dale Quarry beyond. Keep forward until you reach the road at Glebe Farm.

4. Turn left down the road back to the car park. This is where you could end the walk if you wish. Otherwise, walk through the car park and continue along the Trail for Chee Dale and Buxton. You come to the Chee Dale Nature Reserve (another DWT reserve!). Continue along the Trail as it heads under the trees. You reach East Buxton Limekilns, or what remains of them. These were opened in 1880 and worked until 1944, the buttresses being added in the 1920s. You can even go inside one of them.

5. On reaching the bridge which crosses the river Wye, turn right immediately before it (signed 'Monsal Trail via Chee Dale'). Descend to the riverside and turn left. Stay beside the river all the way to the road. As you go look out for water voles. Immediately before the road, turn left through a stile and then left immediately to climb some steps back to Millers Dale Station. At the top turn right and cross to the car park beyond the old station building.

The River Wye at Litton Mill

PLACES OF INTEREST NEARBY

The **church of St John the Baptist** in Tideswell is known as the Cathedral of the Peak and it is easy to see why. It's nice to see that it is open all day too. Alternatively, head for **Buxton** or **Bakewell** and look around these lovely old towns.

ASHFORD IN THE WATER

There is an absolutely stunning view towards the end of this walk, looking down onto the A6 and Ashford in the Water. You will probably want to savour it – and why not? Part of the enjoyment of a walk is just to sit and take it in. Before you get to enjoy the view though there's much more to see in and around Bakewell. In short, this is an exceedingly good walk with plenty of variety.

Walking into Bakewell

- **HOW TO GET THERE:** Follow the A6 west from Bakewell. Turn right for Ashford in the Water after 2 miles and then left into the village itself.
- **PARKING:** In the small car park in the centre of the village: drive towards the church along Church Street from the Ashford Arms Hotel and take the first turn right into Court Lane. The car park is along here on the right. Alternatively park in the village.
- **LENGTH OF WALK:** 6 miles. Map: OS OL24 White Peak Area (GR 194698).

The Ashford Arms is probably one of my favourite local pubs. The food is great and there's a good sized beer garden to enjoy gorgeous summer weather, when it comes along. There is plenty of choice on the menu with specials such as the award winning Olde English sausage served on a bed of mash with onion gravy; lemon pepper chicken; and Thai marlin. There are standard dishes too such as steak, mushroom and ale pie, and fisherman's pie as well as the 'Sizzling Dishes' featuring Hartington chicken. The beers on offer are Black Sheep Bitter, Abbot Ale, Marstons Pedigree and Theakston's Traditional Mild. Opening hours are from 12 noon to 3 pm and from 6 pm to 11.30 pm, except Sunday when they are open all day.

Telephone: 01629 812725.

THE WALK

1. From the car park entrance (with the toilets on your left) turn left on the road. Follow this, keeping the church on your right. Turn left towards the Ashford Arms. Turn right to the main road (the A6020). Cross this and walk along the dead-end road, crossing the river Wye twice to reach the A6. Turn left here for 50 yards and pass through a gate on your left. In the fields, follow the obvious path with the Wye on your left. The path is clear enough before rising up some banking and then descending into a small valley. Rise up the other side to pass through a wicket gate. Stay on the path beyond to cross a road with houses either side. Continue on the path opposite to reach the A6.

2. Turn left and keep going for 500 yards, ignoring a road bridge to your left. Some 300 yards later on your left, have a look at the packhorse bridge (Holme Bridge), but our route continues beside the A6. At Victoria Mill fork left and follow the path between the mill stream on your left and Milford House on your right. Walk beside the stream to reach a road. At the far end (you will see it is Castle Street) keep forward to reach the river Wye again. Keep beside this to Bakewell Park. Continue with the river on your left, looking out for the fish waiting to be fed. In the park, pass behind the cricket pavilion and stay by the river on the grass if you wish, rather than the path. When you have gone as far as you can beside the river walk along the tarmac path (if you aren't already doing so). This will lead you through the children's playground where you reach Holywell, restored by the District Council in 1988. Beyond this you reach the A6.

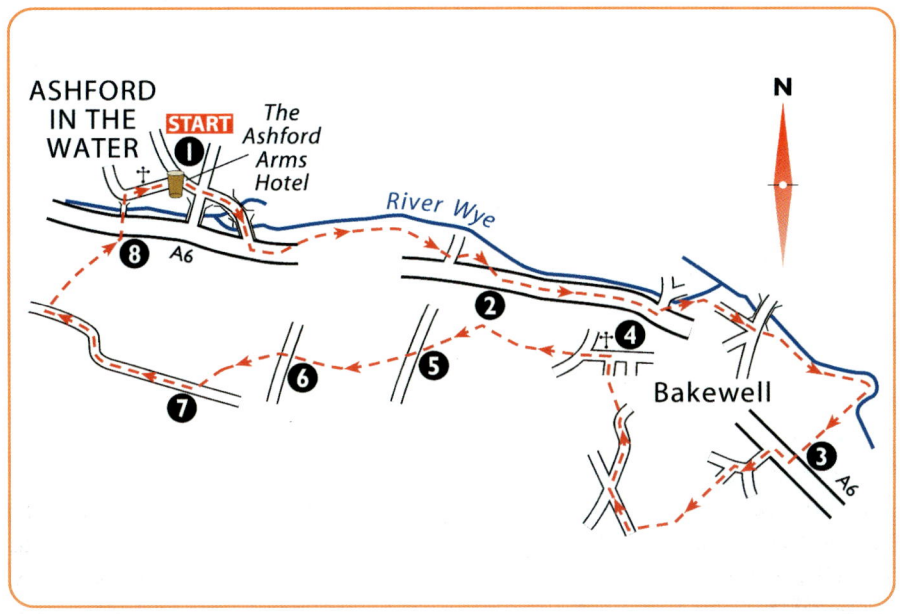

3. Turn right. Then just under 100 yards later turn left into Holywell. Subsequently fork right up Park Road, then left into Park View. Within a few yards turn right on the footpath leading uphill into Catcliff Wood. Climb the steps directly ahead. Continue forward with Bakewell Cemetery on your right. On reaching a gravel track turn right. Keep forward to reach a road with the main cemetery entrance on your right, Immediately beyond bear right down a wide tarmac path beyond some bollards. Follow this downhill as it bears left and then right. Just beyond the right-hand bend take a footpath on your left underneath the beech trees. It is hard to believe you are in the middle of Bakewell. Stay on it to reach the end of the lane. Keep forward to the main road ahead.

4. Cross the road and enter the churchyard. Turn left at the top of the steps, walking up through the churchyard with the church on your right. With the entrance to the church on the right, proceed uphill towards the stone archway with 'Parsonage Croft' signed beyond. (Just before you reach the archway look out for the 'Wildgoose' and 'Willgoofe' gravestones on your left!) Beyond the archway walk up Parsonage Croft. Keep forward to take the footpath between Thorncliffe and The Orchard. As if by magic you find yourself back in the countryside. Walk up the left side of the first field, keeping forward at the wall corner on your left.

Ashford in the Water

Pass through the small gate. In the second field bear half left, keeping in the same direction in the third field (heading for a point to the right of a green-roofed shed). Longstone Edge is away to your right. Stay in the same direction in the narrow fourth field to reach a lane.

5. Turn left here for 10 yards, then right into the field. Head downhill to cross a step-over stile on the left (with a copse of trees on the right). Head towards the stone-roofed barn on the opposite side of the valley. Descend into the grassy valley and rise out of it to pass through a wicket gate in the far left corner of the field. Beyond this walk down the left side of the field to another lane. As you go look across to the far side of the field beyond the lane for the stile you need to aim for shortly.

6. Cross the lane aiming for the stile you saw before. Most walkers seem to follow the track (which is actually slightly to the right of where the public footpath should be) before swinging left to the stile in the hawthorn hedge. Cross the second field, passing through the line of hawthorns, crossing the corner of the third field beyond. Keep in the same direction in the fourth field through a line of hawthorns. In the fifth field climb a grassy bank and climb up some steps in the far corner to reach a lane.

7. Turn right for ⅔ mile, passing Dirtlow Farm as you go. On a left-hand bend (with a mast on the right) pass through a wicket gate on your right, walking towards the mast. The path runs down the right side of the field to bring you to a cottage on the right. There are great views as you walk down this field. Follow the driveway from the cottage to reach the A6.

8. Cross the A6 carefully to reach Sheepwash Bridge opposite. Cross this and find your way back to your car.

PLACES OF INTEREST NEARBY

In Bakewell itself is the **Old House Museum** (telephone: 01629 813642.) As it says on its website, it 'contains a wonderful collection of items from the Bakewell area'. If you travel a couple of miles south-east on the A6 you arrive at **Haddon Hall**, a well-preserved medieval manor house owned by the Manners family, the Dukes of Rutland which has featured in numerous films and TV programmes. Telephone: 01629 812855.

WINCLE AND THE RIVER DANE

The walk from Wincle joins the Gritstone Trail and leads you to Barleigh Ford Bridge where there's time to watch the Dane flow by beneath. A short climb and then you're never far from water as you head back along this lovely wooded valley.

An isolated cottage passed on the way

- **HOW TO GET THERE:** From the A54 south-west from Buxton, shortly after the hairpin bend at Allgreave, turn left at the crossroads for Wincle and Swythamley. On reaching a T-junction turn left for Danebridge.
- **PARKING:** Roadside parking downhill from the Ship Inn.
- **LENGTH OF WALK:** 4 miles, Map: OS OL24 White Peak Area (GR 961652).

You're unlikely to meet many walkers on this route even though it's in the Peak District and quite, quite lovely. Even in the second most visited national park in the world, you can still find some solitude. The route rises from the Ship Inn and when you reach Wincle Grange you may wish to stand and stare (though courtesy demands otherwise!).

It seems strange having a Ship Inn so far from the sea but this may be because 'ship' is a corruption of 'sheep' … well, that's one theory. The Ship Inn, though, is a great pub. It's been extended in the last year or two so there's more space than there used to be. The regular beers are Fullers London Pride and Moorhouses Premium Bitter, with guests such as Pitchfork. Even the sandwich menu here is impressive – how does home-cured ham with tomato and wholegrain mustard mayonnaise strike you? I didn't spot Povey's Staffordshire oatcakes stuffed with local black pudding, cheddar and bacon on the menu until later but I would certainly have tried it. Then, for the more sophisticated perhaps, there's pan-seared Scottish scallops tossed through a fig and parma ham salad … and so it goes. It does get busy here so bear that in mind.

Telephone: 01260 227217.

THE WALK

1. Walk up the road, passing the Ship Inn on your right and 50 yards beyond it look out on your left for some steps in the wall. Climb these off the road. Cross the corner of the first field, heading towards the stile to the right of some buildings. Cross the driveway beyond and climb the steps ahead. Bear left, walking beside a wall on your left. This brings you to a wood. Follow the path up through the trees. At the top, keep forward across a field to the far end of a line of silver birch trees.

2. Climb onto a country lane and walk left. In 200 yards pass a pond on your left. Just before the drive leading into Wincle Grange splits into three, climb a stepover on the left. Walk forward a few yards, then turn right alongside a wall on your right. Continue until you reach a hollow in the field. Climb a stepover and walk diagonally left towards a wall on the far side of the hollow. Proceed with the wall and a line of trees on the left (ignore a farm gate on your left as you go). At the end of the field cross a stepover beside a gate. From here continue on the level, alongside the line of trees straight ahead. You reach two parallel lines of trees. Walk through these. Climb a stepover and turn left, walking along a sunken lane. Keep forward along the track beyond. Then walk

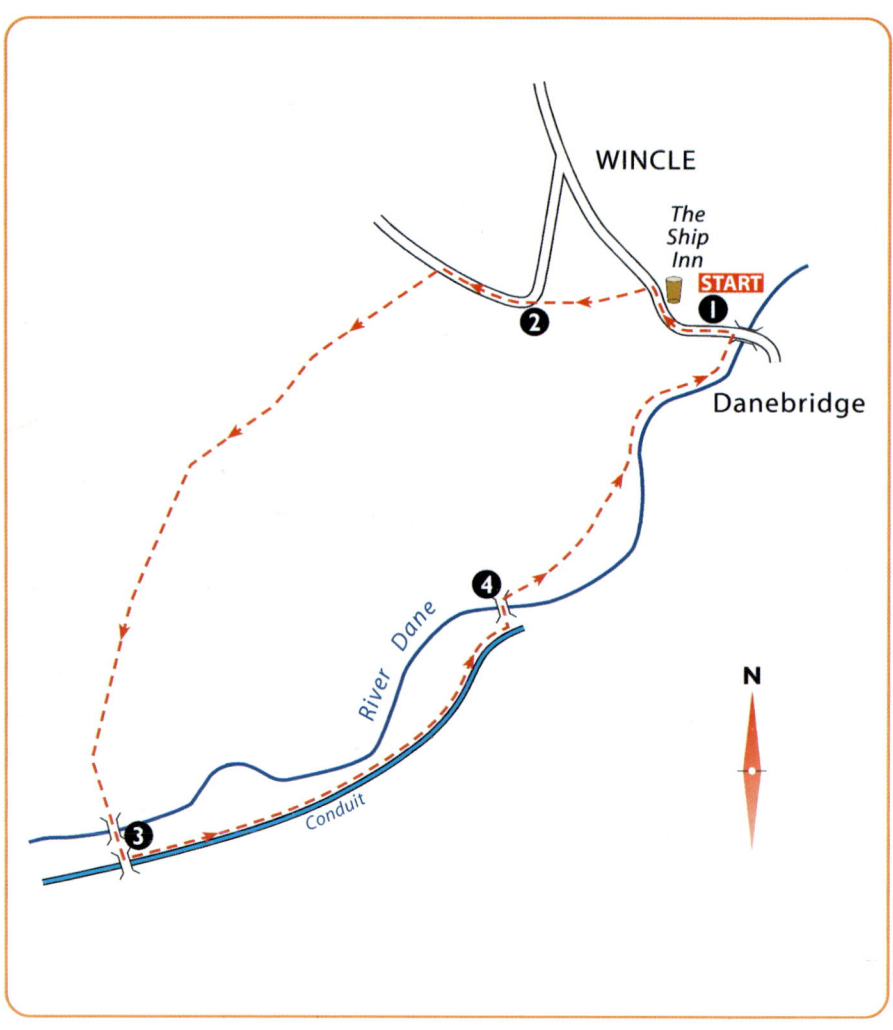

alongside a tree-topped bank on your left. You are now following the Gritstone Trail.

The path comes more out into the open. Ignore a stile on your left. Continue along the grassy track ahead, still beside the banking. Climb a stepover and, 20 yards later, pass through a kissing gate. Continue forward along a well walked path. There should still be a low bank on your left with the ground falling away to the right. Then, with a farm half left of you, the path drops downhill slightly. Cross a number of wooden footbridges as the route picks its way across the hillside. Keep following the 'G' waymarkers. The footpath rises slightly before you descend towards the trees at the end of the field. Enter these trees and on reaching a tarmac driveway, bear right. Cross Barleigh Ford Bridge. Rise up the tarmac driveway.

3. Immediately before another bridge, climb through a squeezer stile on your left. Walk alongside the conduit on the right. You are now following the Dane Valley Way. Stay beside this for some distance. Pass a property on your left and climb a stepover just beyond it. You reach a weir on the left. Cross the footbridge now, following the Dane Valley Way.

The sunken lane

4. On the far side of the river, turn right and walk across the field. Pass through a gateway at the far side of the field, beside the river. Keep forward for 20 yards and then swing left with a wood on your left. Where the field narrows at the far end, pass through a small gate by the river and follow the path with the water on your right. Then pass a stone cottage on the left (Pingle Cottage). On your right are some of the fishing pools of Danebridge Fisheries. Follow the track out of the fisheries. Keeping a number of properties on the left, continue along the concessionary path, along the track to the lane. Turn left back to the car.

PLACES OF INTEREST NEARBY

Tittesworth Reservoir is about 4 miles south-east of Wincle. If you're a birdwatcher there's plenty to see here, and after that you can have a cup of tea in the restaurant and look round the giftshop (telephone: 01538 300400).

ROWSLEY AND THE RIVER DERWENT

A wonderful riverside walk from Rowsley along the Derwent, returning with a climb up to Tinkersley and through beautiful Copy Wood.

The Darley Yew

- **HOW TO GET THERE:** Rowsley is on the A6 between Matlock and Bakewell.
- **PARKING:** Turn into School Lane opposite the Peacock in Rowsley. Park at the roadside beside the Recreation Ground just beyond the bridge.
- **LENGTH OF WALK:** 5¼ miles. Map: OS OL24 White Peak Area (GR 256656).

This is one of my favourite areas, especially the stretch through Rowsley Sidings beside the river. Then there's St Helen's church, where you could spend half an hour or so, easily, looking around the churchyard and admiring the Darley Yew. The route back lulls you into a false sense of security as you stroll in a straight line back to Nanny Goat Crossing, guided by Peak Rail's steam railway. Then you find yourself rising up to Tinkersley … but at least you can get your breath back as you amble through beautiful Copy Wood. Just outside the Peak District, this is Derbyshire walking at its best.

You will see the Grouse and Claret as you walk beside the A6 and like a few other of the pubs mentioned in the book, you can stay there if you like. It's a very busy, popular pub concentrating more on providing food than beer. But beer they do provide – Marstons Smooth and Marstons Pedigree. The menu is extensive and you can even get a breakfast here from 7.30 am if you're so inclined – perhaps you'll have done the walk by then! The main courses include coconut chilli chicken, Somerset pork, Canadian melt, beef with Portobello mushrooms and lamb shoulder. There are salads, vegetarian and pasta dishes, light bites and sandwiches (hot and cold). And I've not even mentioned the specials on the board …. Food is served from 11.30 am until 9.30 pm at the weekend and until 9 pm during the week.

Telephone: 01629 733233.

THE WALK

1. Return to the A6 and turn right. Cross the river Derwent by the road bridge and 100 yards later turn right into Old Station Close. Proceed past the car park on the right and walk as far as you can until a gap on the right leads you into the trees. Follow the (mainly) riverside path all the way down to Nanny Goat Crossing ¾ mile later. This path forms part of the Derwent Valley Heritage Way which runs from near Ladybower Reservoir to Derwent Mouth, 55 miles away, south of Derby.

2. On reaching the edge of the Peak Rail site, bear right alongside the river on the right. On entering the first field keep forward alongside a hedge on your left. Do not follow the river! At the end of the first field, keep forward to the left of a short stretch of hedge ahead. In the third field aim for the stile beside the gate across on the other side of the field. In the fourth field, aim to the right of the stone barn ahead. Beyond that walk along the left side of the fifth field. There's an interesting stone

70

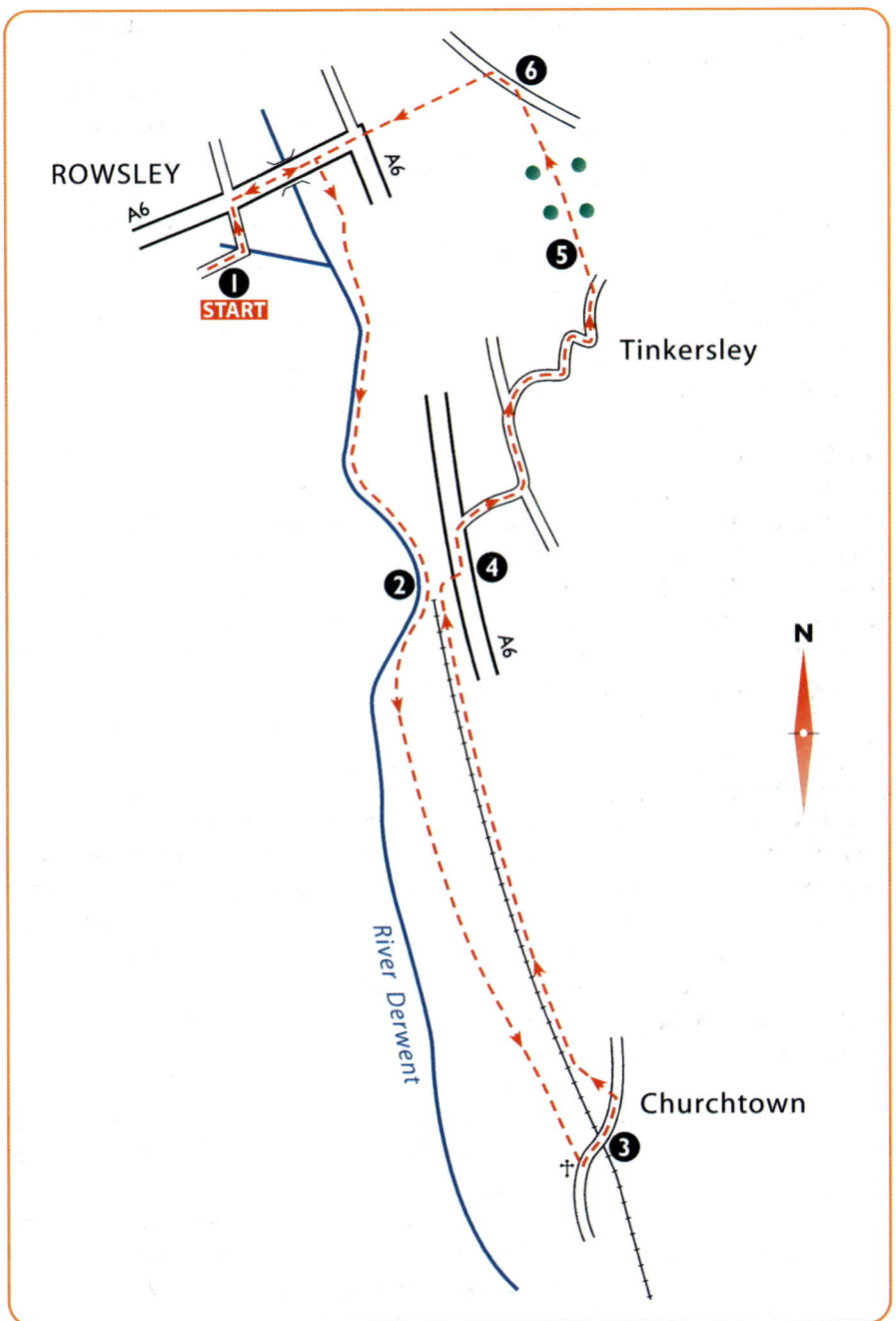

ROWSLEY

A6

A6

START

River Derwent

Tinkersley

A6

Churchtown

N

Rowsley Sidings

step-stile at the end of this field. Walk along the track beyond, ignoring all turns to left and right. You reach a tarmac access road which brings you to Churchtown school on your right. Proceed to the T-junction with St Helen's church to the right. The churchyard is worth visiting for the Darley Yew alone. There aren't many trees that are actually named on an Ordnance Survey map, but the Darley Yew is one of them. It is over 30 ft in circumference and is alleged to be about 2,000 years old! Just stand at its base – you may well be in the presence of the oldest living thing you will ever see in your lifetime.

3. Back on course, turn left along the road. This brings you to Church Road after crossing the railway lane. Just a few yards later, turn left through a gap in the wall and follow the path with the railway line on your left, for a mile or so to reach the car park at the Peak Rail site. Proceed through this to rejoin your outward route at Nanny Goat Crossing. No one seems to know the origin of the name, which is a pity. Turn right up to the A6.

4. Turn left along the A6 and cross at the pelican crossing. Proceed up Northwood Lane, leaving the A6 behind. After 200 yards, as the road does a sharp right turn uphill, turn left. Just beyond the road bridge, look at the old guidepost on your left – it appears to be pointing out the old roads to Bakewell and Matlock. Continue up the quiet lane you are on for 300 yards. Bear right uphill and eventually you reach Tinkersley Farm having zigzagged uphill (first right, then left, another right and finally left). Take the stepover stile beside the gate and keep forward with the property to your right. Cross a stile and walk through the field beyond with the farmhouse above you on the right. The level path brings you to Copy Wood.

5. Enter this wood and proceed along the obvious path ahead. Some 500 yards later you emerge onto what appears to be a small private golf course. Walk across this, keeping on the same level, to reach a step-over stile beside a farm gate.

6. Clamber out onto the road carefully and turn left downhill towards Toll Bar Cottage. Turn left down the path on the far side of the driveway leading to Woodside. Follow this path beside a hedge on your left to enter a field. Keep down the right side of this. At the bottom of this proceed down the obvious path to reach the A6. Continue straight forward along the A6, towards Bakewell, to get back to your car.

PLACES OF INTEREST NEARBY

You're spoilt for choice! Turn left along the A6 and visit **Haddon Hall** (telephone: 01629 812855), or turn right and then left and head up the valley to **Chatsworth House** (telephone: 01246 565300). Both are absolutely stunning properties, but oh so different. Or visit **Peak Rail** (telephone: 01629 580381) by going right along the A6 towards Matlock and then turning right to park in the car park you passed on the walk near Nanny Goat Crossing.

RUDYARD LAKE

A fairly level walk with nothing too taxing. The route encircles Rudyard Lake, which is full of interest all year round. The further you get from the car park, the more peaceful and relaxing this waterside circuit becomes.

The view towards Rudyard Lake

- **HOW TO GET THERE:** Follow the A523 north-westwards from Leek. Take the left turn (the B5331) for Rudyard. After passing under the railway bridge turn left immediately into a car park.
- **PARKING:** Beside Rudyard Lake Steam Railway.
- **LENGTH OF WALK:** 6 miles. Map: OS OL24 White Peak Area (GR 955578).

It is well worth driving to Rudyard to explore this beautiful area. Rudyard is where John Lockwood Kipling met Alice Macdonald in 1863. They were the parents of Rudyard Kipling and the story goes that two years later they named their baby son after the place where they first met. John Lockwood Kipling visited in Victorian times of course, when Rudyard Lake was a well known leisure resort, and it is still massively popular with visitors. The lake was built in the late 18th century to supplement the water in the Caldon and the Trent and Mersey canals.

Many visitors eat at the Rudyard Lake café in the Activity Centre here. In fact, people have been known to travel miles to try their bacon baps. There's only outdoor seating and a small menu but what they provide is tasty and there's nothing like a cuppa after a 6-mile walk. Oh, they also sell Staffordshire oatcakes which are well worth trying. They open from 10 am until about 4 pm though you'll only be able to get those bacon baps until 2 pm or thereabouts. They're open every day from the beginning of April until the end of September, and then only at weekends off season.

Telephone: 01538 306280.

If you fancy something more substantial, visit the Rudyard Hotel on Lake Road nearby.

Telephone: 01538 306208.

THE WALK

1. Walk alongside the narrow gauge railway line on your right. Stay beside it to leave the station behind. Cross the bridge over the B5331. You reach The Dam. Keep straight on. Lakeside Loop is passed. There are some interesting properties across the reservoir on the far side. You then reach Hunthouse Wood where the steam railway appears to end. Keep along the track before passing under first a metal footbridge and then a substantial stone one. A few yards later you reach a small parking area on your right.

2. Swing left here, crossing a stream as you go. Follow a private road leading to Barnes Lea Farm and Cliffe Park Hall. The reservoir may be out of sight before too long. You should now be on the Staffordshire Way and also the Moorlands Walk. The tarmac drive swings right. As you start to climb towards a property at the top of the hill a track forks left into the trees – follow this. The A523 may be visible below the line of trees to your left. The track rises and brings you to the rather grand property

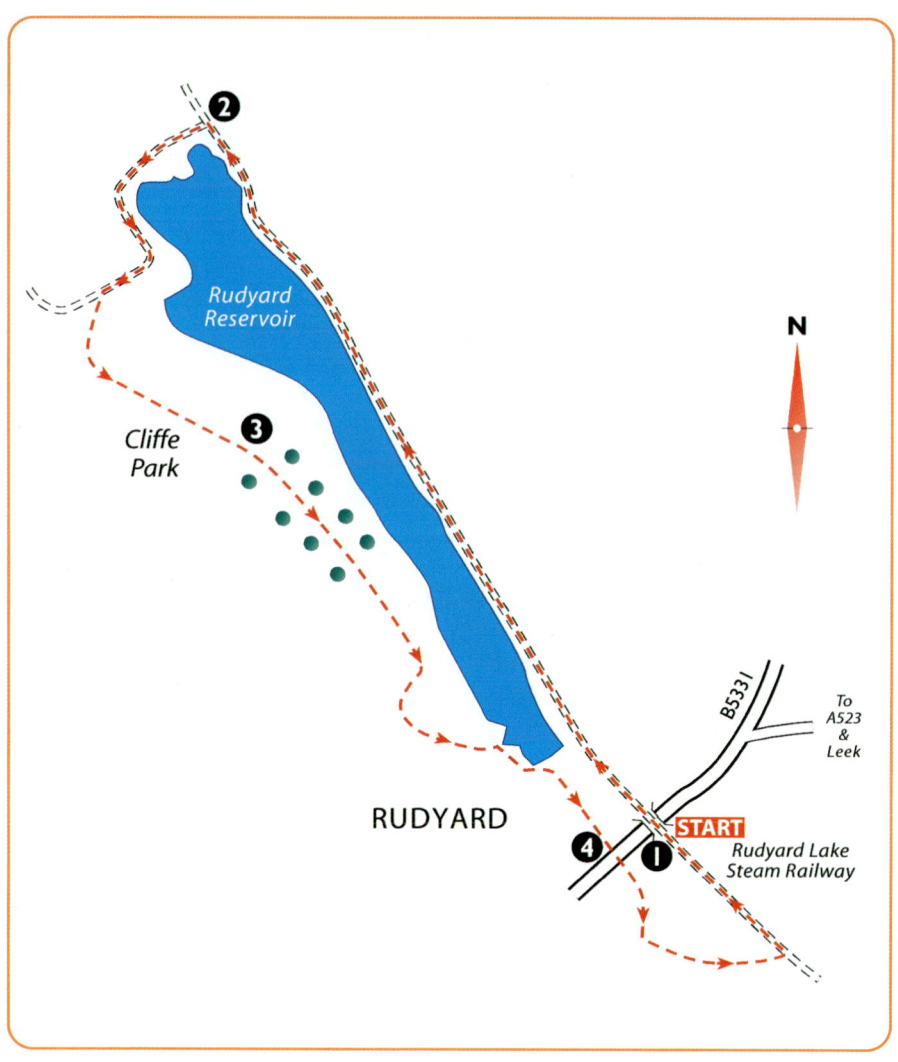

that is Cliffe Park. Here the path goes right through the grounds, keeping the building on your immediate right.

3. Keep forward beyond, along the track to enter Rea Cliffe Wood, with its large and impressive beech trees. Civilisation beckons in the shape of the Rudyard Lake Sailing Club. Proceed along the lane behind it. Stay on this as you pass behind some of the properties you saw earlier from across the lake such as Lady of the Lake, Sandy Point and Sandy Nook.

The way beside Rudyard Lake

Follow the road as it does a right turn and 30 or 40 yards later turn left along a gravel path through the wood. At the far corner of the garden of a red brick property, bear left down a slightly wider gravel path to reach a drive rising uphill from the left. Turn right up the drive. Keep forward until the drive forks and you can follow a public footpath which rises gently into the trees. Bear left when you join another path coming in from the right. This gently bears left and descends downhill. You should still be on the Staffordshire Way. On joining a wide gravel lane, keep forward. On reaching The Crescent on your left, keep forward, bearing right along the road. After 15 yards turn left down a footpath which leads towards the lake. Turn right at the bottom passing the Visitor Centre on your left and the café on your right (you could have your snack now, rather than later, if you wish). Keep past the Visitor Centre toward the drive leading into the parking area. Take the narrow footpath that drops downhill and brings you to the overflow. Proceed alongside the narrower of two watercourses. Keep forward with the stream on your right through a wood.

4. On arriving at a road, cross carefully, continuing along the Staffordshire Way with the stream, actually a canal feeder, on your right. I saw a kingfisher here so look out. On reaching a footbridge on your right stay forward with the feeder still on the right and 500 yards later turn left to climb the steps of the embankment. Turn left back to the car.

PLACES OF INTEREST NEARBY

The Visitor Centre in the converted boathouse gives some interesting information about the lake and its history. Then, of course, it's well worth having a ride on the **Rudyard Lake Steam Railway**, a 3-mile round trip by the side of the lake (telephone: 01995 672280).

Biddulph Grange Garden, a National Trust property approximately 7 miles west of Rudyard Lake is absolutely gorgeous. It is open from mid-March until towards the end of October (usually from Wednesday to Sunday), and then at weekends until the middle of December (telephone: 01782 517999).

DARLEY BRIDGE

A level and easy walk with wonderful scenery and the chance, perhaps, to see a steam train at close quarters before returning alongside the river Derwent to Darley Bridge.

Beside the Derwent

- **HOW TO GET THERE:** Darley Bridge is 2½ miles north-west of Matlock. Follow the B5057 off the A6 in Darley Dale. Cross the railway line and keep straight on at the crossroads. The picnic site is a short distance beyond.
- **PARKING:** Park at Darley Bridge Picnic Site.
- **LENGTH OF WALK:** 4 miles. Map: OS OL24 White Peak Area (GR 269623).

One of the many plus points about waterside walks is that more often than not they aren't too taxing. There are no testing sections at all on this route! So if you're new to walking and not quite sure of your capabilities then this could be the one for you. (It can get a little muddy, though, so be prepared.) The route takes advantage of the concessionary footpath running along the Peak Rail line so there's a long straight walk in towards Matlock when you may get the chance to see one of Peak Rail's steam engines close up. On the way back you'll be following a section of the Derwent Valley Heritage Way. This is largely outside the Peak Park but with this countryside, it wouldn't be amiss if it was all inside.

The Square and Compass pub (passed on the route) is worth visiting if you're looking for a good meal. It's a traditional 18th-century inn, very near the river Derwent, and is open from 5.30 pm during the week, and all day at weekends, from 12 noon. Food includes dishes such as steak, fish, scampi and lasagne, on Sunday a roast is served. Beers on offer include Robinson's Unicorn, Mr Scrooge and Flash Harry.

Telephone: 01629 733255.

When the pub is closed, there are many places to eat in nearby Matlock, or visit the Grouse and Claret at Rowsley (see walk 15).

THE WALK

1. From the picnic site turn right along the road towards the Square and Compass pub. Before you reach it you pass the Darley Dale Cricket Club, which was founded in 1863. Just past the pub, where the road bears right over the bridge, keep forward, taking the right-hand of two squeezer stiles. Walk along the track immediately to the left of the farm buildings. At the end of the track, pass through another squeezer stile and walk beside the wall on your left. Stay beside the wall in the second field. Walk across the middle of the third field. As you enter a fourth field turn left immediately to cross a bridge and follow the path up to the railway line.

2. Don't cross the railway line though! Turn right beside it and walk for 1¼ miles with the track on the left. You come to a bridge over the river Derwent.

3. On the far side of this keep right to reach the path with the river on your right. The path turns right towards Matlock but you should turn left back towards the start. Follow the obvious path for a good ½ mile

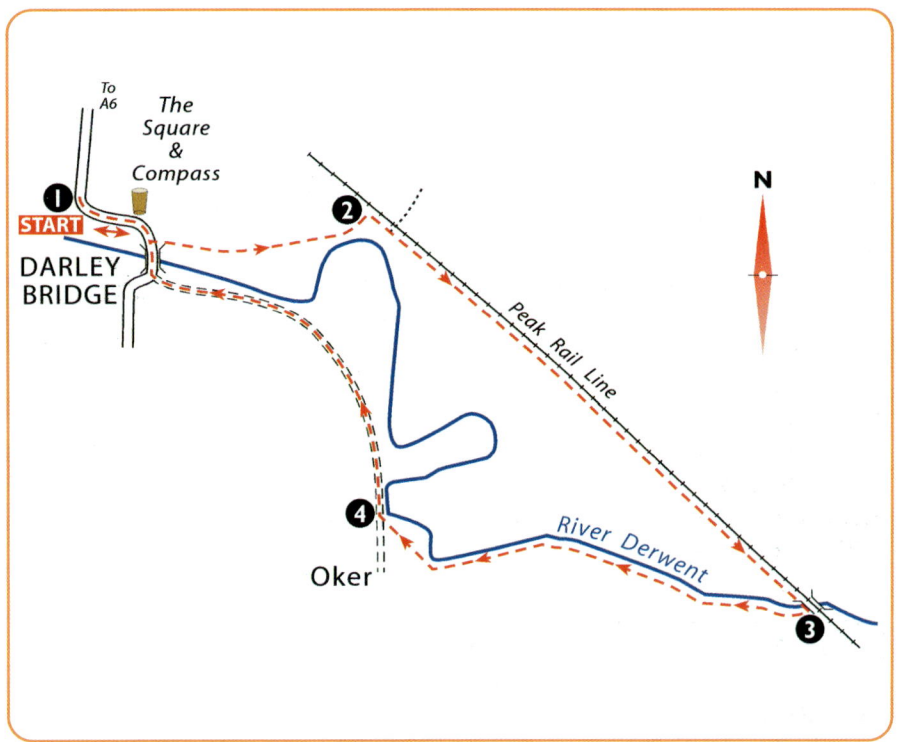

walking. Just beyond the Permanite site keep forward over a farm track that crosses the path to climb a stile and come out into an open field. Follow the clear path in the first field beside the river on your right. Head straight forward in the second field towards the houses ahead. In the third field bear slightly round to the right with the river. Walk up the hedged path into Oker, or should it be Oaker? This is one of those Derbyshire place-names which has two spellings, depending on whether you're a villager or not.

4. Turn right along the lane and stay on it as it becomes more of a track. Ignore all left forks on this track to reach a gate leading into the field. Ignore the track forking right. You should follow the left-hand fork and the Derwent Valley Heritage Way. Stay on this road, looking out for cars occasionally as it is a road open to vehicles. The road brings you through a small group of houses and subsequently into Darley Bridge. Turn right over the river bridge and follow the road all the way back to the picnic site.

The bridge at Darley Bridge

PLACES OF INTEREST NEARBY

Visit **Peak Rail** (telephone: 01629 580381), heading back to Darley Dale station between the picnic site and the A6. If you have young children with you, you could go down to **Matlock Bath** and **Gullivers Kingdom** (telephone: 01925 444888). There is also the **Peak District Mining Museum** in Matlock Bath (telephone: 01629 583834), or go for a cablecar ride up to the **Heights of Abraham** (telephone: 01629 582365).

ALSTONEFIELD AND THE RIVER DOVE

It's doubtful that there's a more stunning walk in the book than this one – the scenery is rather special. Be warned, though, that after walking through the fields away from the village you have to descend about 200 steps to reach the river Dove, but then there's a delightful stroll through beautiful Dovedale to make it worthwhile.

Looking towards Frank-i-th-Rocks Bridge

- **HOW TO GET THERE:** Follow the B5054 south-east from Hartington, turning left at Hulme End for Alstonefield.
- **PARKING:** In the public car park near the George. There is also some roadside parking nearby.
- **LENGTH OF WALK:** 5 miles. Map: OS OL24 White Peak Area (GR 130556).

Stunning Dovedale lies on the border between Derbyshire and Staffordshire. This area can be very busy on summer weekends, many people attracted by the scenery and the chance to cross the river on the famous stepping stones. Towards the end of the walk you'll get the chance to gaze into the murk of Green Well. This was the original source of water for the village and it was used as recently as 1957. I don't know about you but I certainly wouldn't fancy drinking from it!

What can I say about the George that hasn't been said before? This is a gem of a pub. The ambience in the little bar to the right as you enter is second to none, especially when it's full of walkers. The food is delicious – do try the locally reared pork, apple and cider casserole or the fish and chips with home-made mushy peas when they are on the lunch menu, which is available between 12 noon and 2.30 pm. The George is open from 11.30 am until 3 pm during the week and all day at the weekend. It gets very busy on a Sunday! The regular beers are Marstons Pedigree and Marstons Burton Bitter with guests such as Hydes Jekyll's Gold.

Telephone: 01335 310205.

THE WALK

1. Turn right along the road out of the car park. This rises, then bears left (signed 'Lode Mill' and 'Ashbourne'). After 200 yards fork left on the first track, immediately before a small wood.

2. In 400 yards fork right for Gipsy Bank. Stay on the track as it runs along the edge of a number of fields. The track reaches some buildings. Proceed straight through the yard to a small gate and follow the track beyond (keeping on the right side of the field). Away to your left are views of Wolfscote Dale. At the end of the first field pass through the left-hand of a pair of farm gates. Head across the second field towards a small gate to the left of a single tree in the field. Keep in the same direction across the third field, before heading directly towards the dale in the fourth field. This brings you to the National Trust-owned Gipsy Bank. Follow the obvious path ahead. There are some stunning views from here but watch out underfoot. If you want to count the steps, perhaps someone could get back to me with the number!

3. Cross the bridge over the Dove (or use the original stepping stones if you want some excitement). Turn left to walk upstream beside the river on your left and 300 yards later ignore the path to the right into

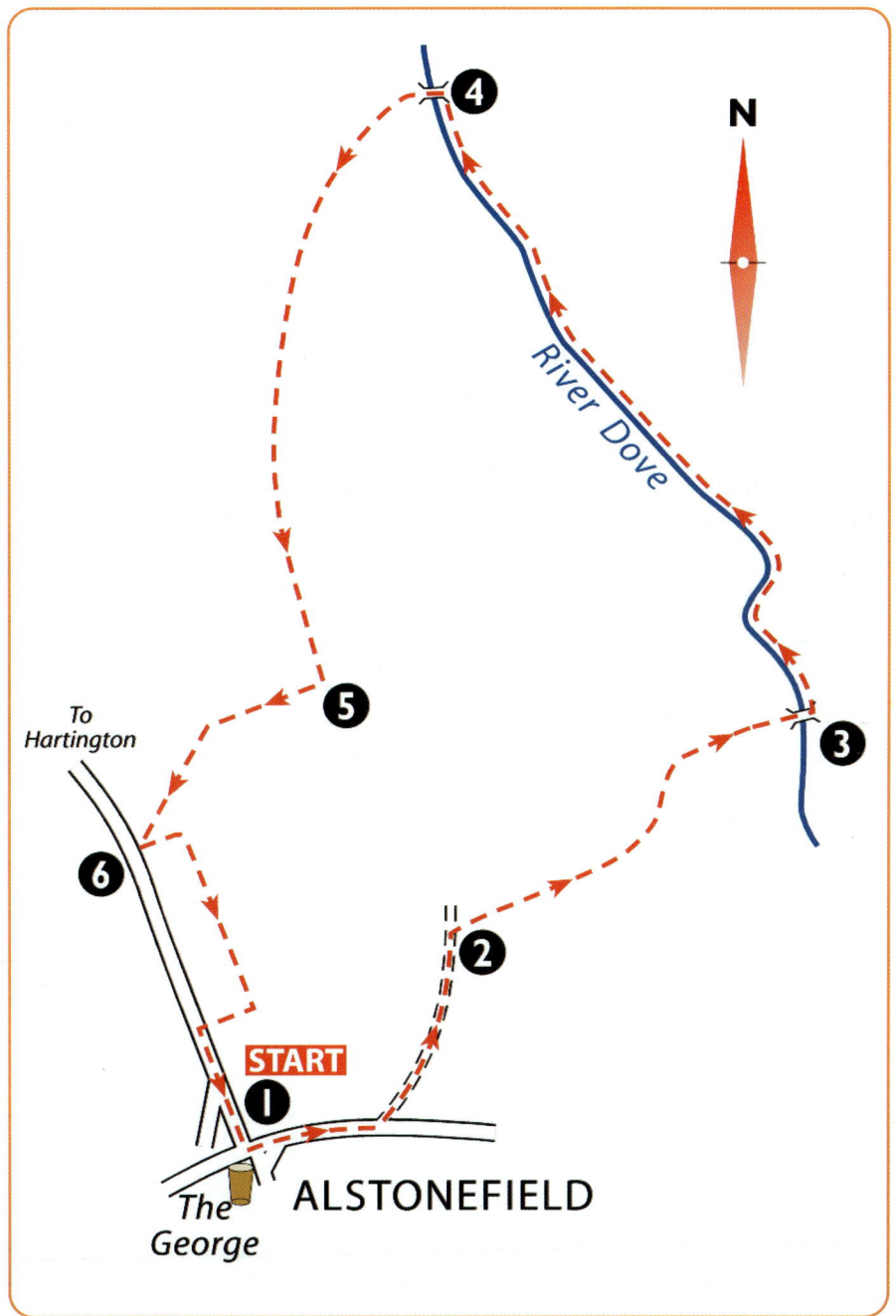

N

River Dove

To
Hartington

4

3

5

6

2

START

1

The
George

ALSTONEFIELD

Walking towards Narrowdale Hill

Biggin Dale, stay beside the Dove. It is likely to be very busy hereabouts on a warm Sunday!

4. A good mile later you reach a bridge on your left which is known (apparently) as Frank-i-th-rocks Bridge. Cross the bridge, bearing right beyond with the river now on your right. You will see you are on National Cycleway No 54 as well as the Sabrina Way. Pass through a gate and proceed on the gravel path as it swings left away from the Dove. The path rises slightly above the marshy ground on the right where on the far side is Beresford Dale. You may even get a glimpse of a tower on the rocks above the dale. Where Cycleway 54 swings right through a gate you should turn left along a stone track which leads in the general direction of Narrowdale Hill, 367m above sea level. Keep on the track for about ½ mile until the track swings right towards the farm (known as Narrowdale). Keep forward at the right-hand turn through a stile beside a gate into the field beyond. This takes you into a shallow dry dale which you should gradually climb. Enter the access land, keeping straight forward alongside a wall on the right. You should be heading for Low Plantation on the hill in front. There is then a gap in the wall ahead but keep forward to proceed up the right side of it. A steepish climb brings you to the top of the field.

5. Turn right for 20 yards and cross a stile. Proceed along the walled track beyond. It sweeps right towards a cottage but 100 yards before the cottage turn left for 'Alstonfield' (sic). The path heads towards the far left corner of a wood. Continue in the same direction through two more fields to reach a road.

6. Do not climb onto the road. Turn sharp left, walking alongside a wall on your right. Just beyond a tumbled down building turn right over a stile. Then keep forward towards Alstonefield to cross a stile on the far side of the field. Keep forward, heading just to the left of the village ahead through a number of fields to reach a track directly in front of a building. Turn right on the track to a lane. Turn left, passing a grass triangle to the main road. A few yards later on the opposite side of the road is Green Well. Keep on the road back to the car park.

PLACES OF INTEREST NEARBY

The church and churchyard at **Alstonefield** are worth a visit. At the back of the church must be one of the oldest gravestones in the country, dating back to the early 16th century. **Milldale** and **Ilam** are both nearby and interesting to stroll around – the first with Viator's Bridge and the latter with St Bertram's Well, amongst other things.

GRINDON AND THE MANIFOLD WAY

Set out from Grindon, a quiet, attractive limestone village in the south of the Peak District, and before you know it you are surrounded by gorgeous scenery in the valley of the river Manifold, with so many features to enjoy.

Thor's Cave

- **HOW TO GET THERE**: Grindon is 5 miles south-west of Hartington. Take the B5053 south-westwards from there and then look for a sign for Grindon to the left.
- **PARKING**: In the small car park behind the churchyard in Grindon (and it is small).
- **LENGTH OF WALK**: 6½ miles. Map: OS OL24 White Peak Area (GR 084545).

It has to be said that this may be a waterside walk with no water at certain times of the year and when you get to the Manifold Way you will be able to see whether the river is running above ground or has temporarily dried up. But this is still gorgeous Peak District scenery – a bit more strenuous than some of the other walks but you can look up at the dramatic Thor's Cave and wonder how ancient man managed to survive up there thousands of years ago, and admire the work done by the National Trust in conserving this wonderful landscape.

Getting to the Wetton Mill Tea Room can be part of the day's adventure, a chance to explore this area. Drive north-west to the village of Butterton and pass through the cobbled ford before rising up to the church at the top end of the village. Then turn right and then right again to drop back down to the valley and Wetton Mill. The tea room sells sandwiches, cakes, teacakes, crumpets and toast. Snacks in other words, and of course, most importantly, you can get a refreshing cup of tea here. It is in a lovely setting, however, and you can always have your main meal later. It opens every day from 10 am until 5 pm, from the beginning of April until the end of October but then probably only on Sunday the rest of the year.

Telephone: 01298 84838.

THE WALK

1. From the car park, walk back the way you have driven, with the church to your left. Turn right at the T-junction of lanes. Then bear left at the large-ish grass triangle. Keep left at the end of it. This takes you downhill. On the right used to be the Cavalier Inn. Bear right on the dead end road, passing a pinfold on your left almost immediately. Then bear left along a track in front of a bungalow (Hurdon Lowe). Bear right at the end of the bungalow and continue down the track. Ignore another track to the left about 100 yards later.

2. Approximately 10 yards later turn left through the wall, taking a path to the right which runs parallel to the track you were on. Continue, passing through various stiles and a gate, for 500 yards to reach a field with a couple of tumbled-down buildings at the far end. In this field, in the far right corner, pass through a squeezer stile back onto the track. Keep forward to reach an open field. At this point, proceed along the grassy track. The Manifold Valley is to your left, providing glorious views. At the end of the field cross a step-over stile and continue down the right

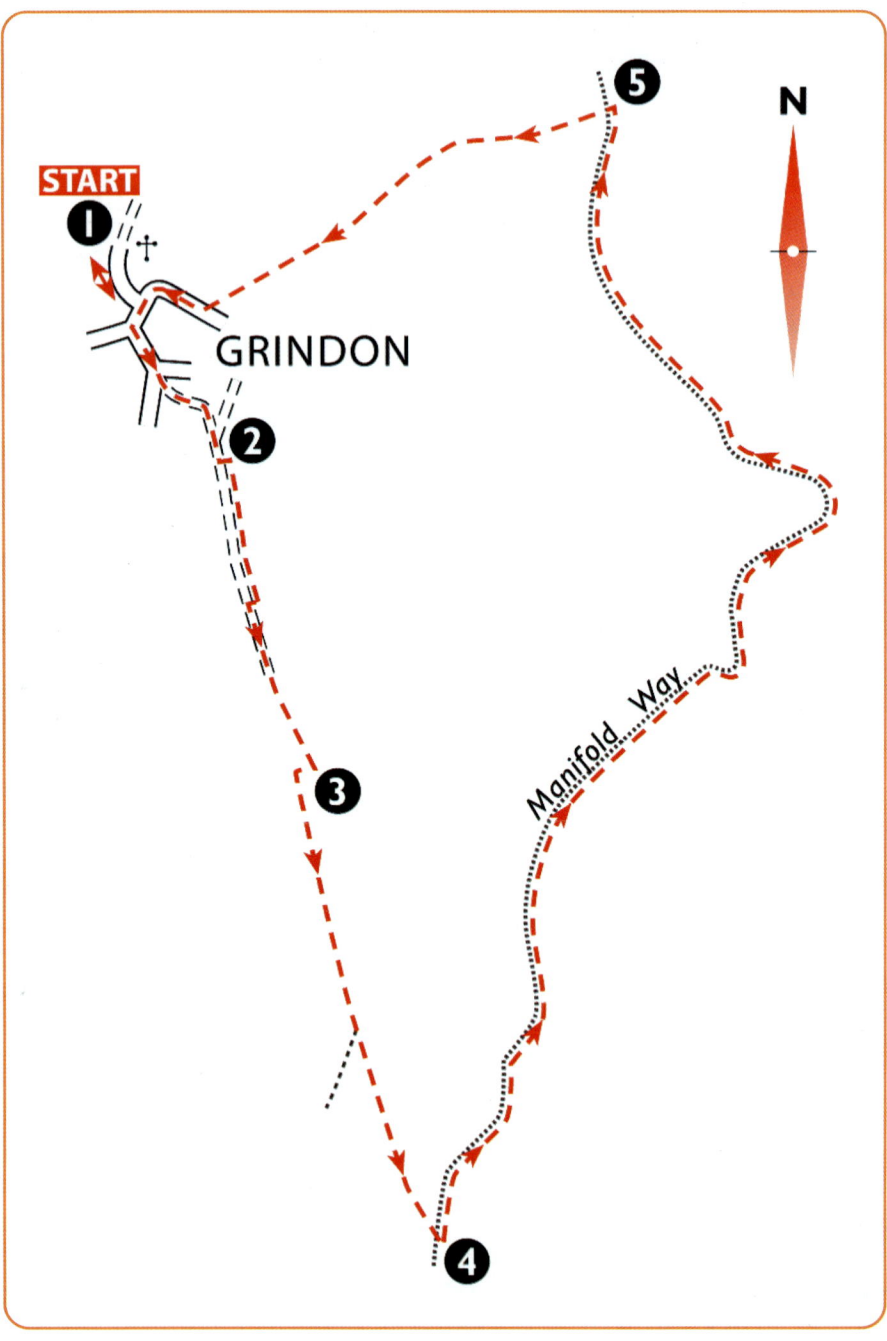

START

1

GRINDON

2

3

4

5

N

Manifold Way

side of the next field. Then pass through a gateway and follow the track as it descends into the valley before rising to the buildings ahead.

3. Walk directly through the farm. Proceed on the driveway beyond. Nearly 700 yards later on a slight right-hand bend, the driveway descends slightly. Don't follow it! Keep forward through a bridlegate. Keep straight forward along the left side of the wall. There's a benchmark on the frame of the gate you've just passed through. Keep forward to another bridlegate. Beyond this pass the stone barn to your left and keep forward to reach a stone step-stile. Then keep forward through the next two fields to pass through another bridlegate, bearing left a few yards later passing through another gate. In the field beyond proceed to the right of a barn ahead and 20 yards after this a (sometimes muddy) track takes you under the trees into the next field. Keep forward through the gateway ahead, then a kissing gate, to reach the Manifold Way.

4. Turn left along the Manifold Way and see if the river Manifold is running. Lee House Farm Tea Room is on your right as you go. Time for a cuppa ? Stay on the Manifold Way for the next 3 miles. As you go, the river (assuming it's running) will swing from one side of you to the other. As you proceed, remember at Weag's Bridge to keep forward along the Manifold Way, crossing the lane that crosses the bridge on your right.

5. Eventually Thor's Cave looms up above you. Just beyond this, round the corner, on your left, a path leads into Ladyside Wood. Follow the path into the trees and start your ascent. The path zigzags upwards. You come out into the open. Pass through the line of hawthorns and beyond keep alongside the fence on your left. You should be level with Thor's Cave by now. On reaching a step-over stile on your left, turn left into the wood and follow the clear path through the trees. A stile leads into a more open area. Stay beside the fence past the National Trust sign to reach a water trough. Climb the squeezer stile to the left of this and climb the grassy bank beyond, bearing slightly left to rise to the higher ground ahead. The houses of Grindon should soon be visible, and the church spire. At the far end of the field, pass through a wicket gate and cross a footbridge. Head up to the stile at the top of the rise. Cross this and head directly away from it to the left of the tallest trees in front. Pass through a squeezer stile by a farm gate to reach a lane. Turn right towards the church. Look out for the Rindle Stone, near the church gate. Return to your car.

A pheasant encountered on the route

PLACES OF INTEREST NEARBY

Five miles southwest is the RSPB's **Coombes Valley** (telephone 01538 384017) where there are birds to watch, or drive south to **Waterhouses** on the A523 and hire a bicycle to ride along the Manifold Way – telephone 01538 308609 for more details. They aren't open all the year round, so please check beforehand.

ILAM AND THE RIVER DOVE

This easy walk is largely on National Trust property, and spans two counties. Near Ilam the rivers Manifold and Dove meet and there are great views all the way.

Cottages in the village of Ilam

- **HOW TO GET THERE:** Ilam is approximately 4½ miles north-west of Ashbourne.
- **PARKING:** At the National Trust car park at Ilam Hall. As you enter, take note of the whereabouts of the church.
- **LENGTH OF WALK:** 3½ miles. Map: OS OL24 White Peak and OS Explorer 259 Derby (GR 131507).

Starting from Ilam, a unique estate village in Staffordshire, you reach Coldwall Bridge on the Derbyshire side of the border – you may be surprised by how impressive this is. It was obviously a much more important river crossing a few hundred years ago than it is now. The return journey (in Staffordshire) gives splendid views to bring you back into Ilam.

The Manifold Tearoom is a lovely place to have a snack and recharge your batteries. Sit outside on a warm summer's day and admire that view. Try the oatcakes, jacket potatoes, home-made soup, or the luxury cakes. In the winter it is only open at the weekend but from Easter to October it opens from Friday to Tuesday, 11 am until 5 pm.

Telephone: 01335 350245.

THE WALK

1. From the car park, walk to the church. Proceed along the gravel path with the church on your right. Beyond the churchyard bear left along the wider gravel path which leads into Ilam village. On reaching the entrance to Dovedale House on the left, bear right, then right again, to walk alongside the road through the village.

2. On reaching the memorial to Mary Watts Russell (wife of a former estate owner) in the middle of the road near the bridge, bear left for Dovedale and Thorpe. Just beyond the last house on your left, pass through the wicket gate. Bear right up the path to join a track. Turn right along this and you reach a seat which has been placed there in memory of 'Bill Hudson who farmed the land around here for almost 50 years'. At the end of the first field there is a marvellous view of Thorpe Cloud, the flat-topped hill in front. In the second field, head towards Thorpe Cloud, and pass through a small swing gate into the third field. Here again head in the general direction of Thorpe Cloud. On your left is Bunster Hill. Cross the narrow fourth field, aiming for Thorpe Cloud in the fifth field. Cross one of a pair of step stiles and walk through the trees beyond. Then keep forward in the same direction to reach a tarmac lane. Turn left on the lane, passing a toilet block on your right. Turn right off the lane to cross a footbridge over the river Dove.

3. Immediately beyond the bridge, turn right over a stile. Head across the field on an obvious path to then reach the Dove on your right. Follow this to walk beside a riverside woodland. Look out for dippers in the river around here. Once out of the trees bear right to the wicket gate

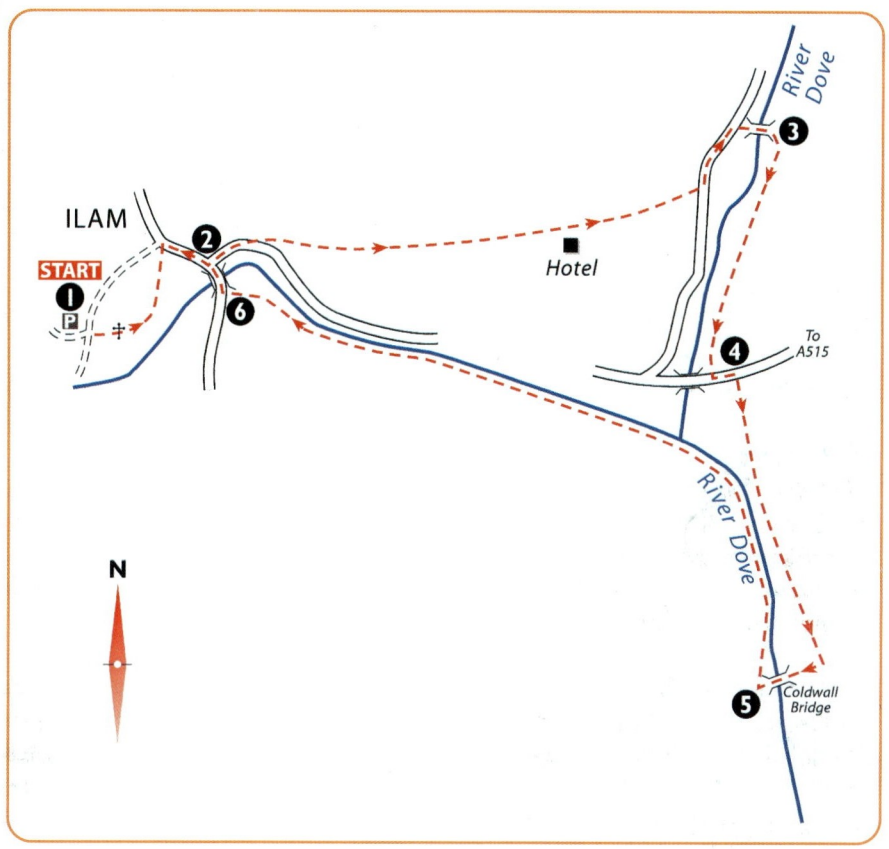

across the field. Pass through another wicket gate and keep forward beside a broken line of trees on your right. You reach the road that crosses St Mary's Bridge, to your right.

4. Turn left for a few yards and then right into the field. Follow the path across the field, crossing a step-over by a gate. Keep forward beyond, crossing a boggy area by a concrete slab and keeping to the left of a stream. Stay beside the stream to pass through a wicket gate. Walk through a narrow enclosure which opens out as you go. You join the river Dove. Follow this, keeping it on your right, until you reach Coldwall Bridge just under ½ mile later.

5. Cross the bridge, but a few yards before the end pass through a squeezer stile on your right and follow the path out of the trees. Then

Looking towards Thorpe Cloud

keep parallel to the hedge/fence at the bottom of the field to reach and pass through a gate. Keep on the track beyond, keeping forward straight ahead (and uphill) as the track swings left. Stay 30 yards or so away from the fence on your right. The path gets a little nearer the fence but after crossing a grassy ditch (which may be all that remains of an old hedgerow) keep forward until you reach a point where the fence bears right downhill. You should do the same but within a few yards, a clear path will take you away from the fence as you descend steadily. The path leads you to a stile which brings you to a riverside field. Cross this and follow the path back to the road bridge in Ilam. In the last field before the lane the path actually crosses the field directly from one stile to the other beside the bridge – it seems that a lot of walkers stick to the riverside however.

6. Turn right over the river and then left to walk back to the car park at Ilam Hall.

PLACES OF INTEREST NEARBY

Ashbourne is an interesting town. The Green Man and Blacks Head is said to have had the longest inn sign in the world. To give it its full title, it used to be known as 'The Royal Green Man and Blackamoor's Head Commercial and Family Hotel'. The inn sign still stretches right across the road – check it out. St Oswald's church is well worth looking around too. If you happen to be hereabouts on Shrove Tuesday or Ash Wednesday you may (or may not!) fancy visiting Ashbourne to watch one of the most unusual games of 'football' in the world. It takes place in the town and the goals are some 3 miles apart.